A Mozart Legacy

A Mozart Legacy

Aspects of the British Library collections

Alec Hyatt King

University of Washington Press   Seattle

To the memory of
Cecil Bernard Oldman
(1894–1969)

© 1984 The British Library Board

Library of Congress Catalog Card Number   84-051990

ISBN 0-295-96201-1

Designed by James Shurmer

Typeset by Channel Eight Ltd., Bexhill-on-Sea

Printed in England by The Pitman Press, Bath

Contents

Acknowledgements

For permission to reproduce non-copyright illustrations from collections other than those owned by the British Library Board, thanks are due as follows: to the Trustees of the British Museum (pl.I, II; figs.1, 2, 3, 4, 8, 17, 18, 25); to the Heirs of Stefan Zweig (figs.27, 28, 29, 30, 34); to the Internationale Stiftung Mozarteum, Salzburg (figs.10, 13). The following illustrations are reproduced by permission of the copyright holders: Bärenreiter Verlag, Kassel (fig.43); Breitkopf & Härtel, Wiesbaden (figs.39, 41).

Preface

In 1956 the British Museum mounted a large Mozart exhibition to mark the bicentenary of the composer's birth, and to accompany it the Trustees published a short illustrated booklet, *Mozart in the British Museum*, which included a summary list of all the exhibits. The booklet was reprinted four times by 1976, but has now been out of print for some time. In certain respects it has also become outdated, mainly because of the rapid progress of Mozart research in the last three decades. Some of the results of this research, particularly as it bears on the study of the autographs of Mozart and his father, are taken into account in the present book, which is more comprehensive and more copiously illustrated than its predecessor.

When, in 1946, the British Museum acquired the Paul Hirsch Music Library, its collection of Mozart's printed music – already of considerable distinction – was much enhanced because Hirsch had made a speciality of Mozart. Since then the representation of Mozart's printed music in the former library collections of the British Museum (which were transferred to the British Library Board in 1973) has grown steadily and substantially by purchase and by copyright deposit. In quantity and variety this collection is now one of the best in any national library in the world, and its rich holding of scarce first editions and other Mozart rarities is now unrivalled except in Vienna.

The number of Mozart autographs and important copies of various kinds now in the British Library's collections has grown little since 1956. While the number of autographs, some thirty-six in all, is not large, many are of high quality. The majority are in the Department of Manuscripts, where their presence is due to generous past bequests, to some judicious purchases in the nineteenth century, and to a loan made by a private collector. Their total has been augmented quite recently by a few important purchases and by another welcome loan, from the Royal College of Organists. Recent, too, was the chance discovery of an important Mozart autograph, which had lain, miscatalogued and so wrongly identified, in a volume of Hummel autographs purchased a century ago.

The reason why this assemblage of Mozart manuscripts is not numerous is a simple one. As explained later in these pages, the bulk of his autograph music, letters and other documents passed, in the course of the nineteenth century, into institutional and national libraries in Austria and Germany. The quantity which was scattered and ultimately found its way into private hands was relatively small, and it was from this that such later accumulations as that now in the British Library took shape.

These manuscripts, then, taken in conjunction with the extensive holding of Mozart's printed music and the large collection of books about him, form a rich resource for study and research.

It is now 218 years since Wolfgang Amadeus Mozart and his father visited the British Museum, towards the end of their long and memorable stay in London, and made their gift to the recently formed institution which, however inchoate, was then already famous. Mozart remained a life-long admirer of England. Were he to return today, we may hope that he would be gratified that so much of his music had been preserved in its national collection.

Alec Hyatt King
London, November 1983

Plate I

British Museum, view of the courtyard, looking south-west. Water-colour by Wykeham Archer. 1842.
230 × 350mm.

Plate II

Leopold Mozart, with his son Wolfgang and his daughter Nannerl. Water-colour by Louis Carrogis de Carmontelle. 1763. 360 × 235mm.

Plate III

A view of Salzburg. Unsigned aquatint. 1807. 282 × 425mm.

Plate IV

Design for *Die Zauberflöte*, Act II, Scene 7. Aquatint by Karl Friedrich Thiele after Karl Friedrich Schinkel. 1823. 348 × 510mm.

List of Illustrations

Colour plates

I. Water-colour of the courtyard of the British Museum. 1842. British Museum, Department of Prints and Drawings, 1914–2–6–28.

II. Water-colour of Leopold Mozart, with his children. 1763. British Museum, Department of Prints and Drawings, BM 1972 U.653.

III. 'Première vue de Salzbourg', *Douze vues du pays de Salzbourg*, no.1. Dom. Artaria, Mannheim, 1807. British Library, Map Library, 7 Tab. 64 (3).

IV. Design for *Die Zauberflöte* by K. F. Schinkel, from his *Decorationen auf den beiden Königlichen Theatern in Berlin*, Heft 3, Berlin, 1823. British Library, Department of Printed Books, 1899. c. 5.

Monochrome illustrations

1. Engraving of the Hon. Daines Barrington. British Museum, Department of Prints and Drawings, C.V. (sub.1). Period 4. Q. 3–57.

2. Engraving of James Harris. British Museum. Department of Prints and Drawings, De Vesme/Calabi no.834, 1891–4–14–82.

3. Mezzotint of Thomas Birch. British Museum, Department of Prints and Drawings, Cheylesmore 1902–10–11–1233.

4. Engraved view of Montagu House. Published by John Bowles, London, 1714. British Museum, Department of Prints and Drawings, Crace XXVIII sheet 31 no.74.

5. *The Microcosm of London*, text by William Henry Penn and William Combe, engravings by Thomas Rowlandson and Augustus Charles Pugin, vol.1, pl.14, 'The Hall and Stair Case, British Museum', R. Ackermann, London, 1808. British Library, Department of Printed Books, 190.e.l.

6. The first edition of Mozart's sonatas for violin and piano, K6,7. Paris, 1764. British Library, Music Library, K.10.a.17.(1).

7. Mozart's *God is our Refuge*. Autograph. 1765. British Library, Music Library, K.10.a.17.(3).

8. Engraving of Leopold Mozart with his children. 1764. British Museum, Department of Prints and Drawings, 1925–2–14–4.

9. Engraving of Leopold Mozart, frontispiece to the Dutch translation of his *Violinschule*, published as *Grondig onderwys in het behandelen der viool*, Haarlem, 1766. British Library, Music Library, Hirsch I. 420.

10. The British Museum's receipt, 19 July 1765, given to Leopold Mozart. Internationale Stiftung Mozarteum, Salzburg.

11. Engraving of Vincent Novello. British Library, Department of Manuscripts, Add. MS 35027 f.36r.

12. Woodcut of Johann Andreas Stumpff. British Library, Department of Printed Books. *Die Gartenlaube,* no.32, 1857, p.437. P.P. 4736. ib.

13. Miniature of Constanze Mozart. Internationale Stiftung Mozarteum, Salzburg.

14. Figured bass progressions by Leopold Mozart. Autograph. British Library, Department of Manuscripts, Add. MS 14396, f.14r.

15. Copy, by Laurent Lausch, of Mozart's concert rondo, 'Al desio, di chi t'adora', K577, preceded by the recitative 'Giunse al fin' from *Le nozze di Figaro.* British Library, Department of Manuscripts, Add. MS 14396 f.21v.

16. Mozart's Duet sonata in B flat major, K358/186c. Autograph. British Library, Department of Manuscripts, Add. MS 14396, f.27r.

17. Engraving of Mozart. British Museum, Department of Prints and Drawings, 1864–6–11–51.

18. Engraving of Franz Joseph Haydn. British Museum, Department of Prints and Drawings, Burney K67.–219.

19. The first edition of Mozart's string quartets, K387, 421/417b, 428/421b, 458, 464, 465. Artaria, Vienna, 1785. British Library, Music Library, R.M. 11.g.17.(1).

20. *Sammlung von Aussichten der Residenzstadt Wien, gezeichnet und gestochen von Karl Schütz und von Johann Ziegler.* Pl.VI, 'Ansicht vom Graben gegen den Kohlmarkt'. Artaria, Vienna, 1798. British Library, Map Library, 183.s.l.

21. Mozart's String quartet in C major, K465. Autograph. British Library, Department of Manuscripts, Add. MS 37763, f.57r.

22. Mozart's String quartet in A major, K464. Autograph. British Library, Department of Manuscripts, Add. MS 37763, f.54v.

23. Mozart's String quartet in G major, K387. Autograph. British Library, Department of Manuscripts, Add. MS 37763, f.6v.

24. A collection of views of Berlin, etc., without titlepage. No.44. British Library, Department of Printed Books, 118.c.1.

25. Silverpoint drawing of Mozart. Reproduced from a photogravure published by the Photographische Gesellschaft in Berlin from the original, 75 × 62 mm, in the Musikbibliothek der Stadt Leipzig. British Museum, Department of Prints and Drawings, 1905–10–19–51.

26. Mozart's String quartet in D major, K575. Autograph. British Library, Department of Manuscripts, Add. MS 37765, f.1r.

27. Mozart's Horn concerto in E flat major, K447. Autograph. British Library, Department of Manuscripts, Loan. 42/7, f.6v of the second foliation.

28. Mozart's Five contredances for orchestra, K609. Autograph. British Library, Department of Manuscripts, Loan 42/11, f.1r.

29. Mozart's autograph sketch of 'Non so più' in *Le nozze di Figaro.* British Library, Department of Manuscripts, Loan 42/8, f.1r.

30. Mozart's autograph thematic catalogue. British Library, Department of Manuscripts, Loan 42/1, ff.18v, 19r.

1. The Mozart Gift

Among all the music by the great masters of the classical period now in the Reference Division of the British Library, the Mozart collections enjoy the unique distinction of having originated in a personal connection between the composer and the British Museum. The connection dates from the summer of 1765, when, towards the end of their long stay in London, the Mozart family paid a special visit to the Museum. This occasion, the important gift of his son's music which Leopold Mozart made to the Trustees, and all the attendant circumstances, form a most interesting episode in the composer's remarkable childhood.

How was it that in 1765 Leopold and his wife found themselves in London with their children, some 800 miles from their native Salzburg, when Wolfgang was less than nine and a half years old and his sister Maria Anna (generally known, until her marriage in 1784, as 'Nannerl') barely fourteen? London was the farthest point in their protracted, hazardous journey which lasted from June 1763 to November 1766, and they stayed there for nearly fifteen months, far longer than in any of the numerous other cities they visited. The Mozart family undertook this journey because Leopold Mozart considered it a divinely ordained duty for him to foster his son's extraordinary genius – 'the miracle which God let be born in Salzburg'. He rightly saw that such talents would be stunted if confined to the narrow, stifling world of the Archbishop's court where he himself held an appointment as second violinist and deputy *Kapellmeister*. Only travel could give the child the widest possible range of musical experience, and ultimately perhaps secure an appointment worthy of his brilliance. So this prodigious journey, which Leopold planned and executed with such skill and resource, is the very embodiment of the first part of Bacon's aphorism: 'Travel, in the younger sort, is part of education: in the elder, a part of experience'. While Mozart made many other journeys in his short life, probably none left a deeper impression on him than that which brought him to London. Travel also gave him a lasting sense of superiority. Twelve years later, in 1778, he wrote to his father from Paris: 'I assure you that people who do not travel (I mean those who cultivate the arts and learning) are indeed miserable creatures'.

A detailed account of the Mozarts' stay in London lies beyond the scope of these pages. But we must know something of their remarkable musical and social activity before we can trace the probable chain of events which ultimately brought about the family's visit to the British Museum. Within five days of their arrival, King George III and Queen Charlotte invited them to court, where Wolfgang and his sister, an excellent harpsichordist, performed, both by themselves and with musicians of the royal household. This was the first of several such visits, and early in 1765 the Queen graciously accepted the fulsome dedication (written by Leopold, in French) of the child's new set of sonatas op.III (K10–15). Having gained royal patronage, Leopold took enormous trouble, in his own words, 'to win over the aristocracy': his travel diaries include the names of various ambassadors and many other important members of the nobility and gentry prominent at court and in the highest social circles. He went to musical soirées, organised concerts under aristocratic patronage, at which Wolfgang's works, among them some new symphonies, were heard, and arranged for him to give at least one special performance for charity. All this took up a lot of time. Throughout the family's sojourn Leopold also arranged a regular succession of exhibition performances, given at various concert rooms and inns, and latterly at their lodgings. On payment of an admission charge the public was invited to see and hear the 'prodigies of

1. The Hon. Daines Barrington (1727–1800). Engraved by C. Knight after J. Slater. 1795. 222 × 180mm.

nature' (as the children were described in the newspapers) perform at the keyboard.

Such hectic activity lasted well into the summer of 1765. But whatever the occasion, and even if Nannerl participated, it was always Wolfgang – being five years younger – who was the main attraction. He was noticed much more, however, as a performer than a composer. No one in London seems to have paid any attention to the nature of his genius until June, when the Honourable Daines Barrington (fig.1) attempted to investigate it. Barrington, son of the second Viscount, was eminent as a lawyer, antiquary and man of science, in the widest sense of the term. He was also an amateur musician and author of one of the earliest and most thorough studies of birdsong in English. Having heard Wolfgang play at some public concerts, he then visited the family in their lodgings at 20 Thrift (now Frith) Street, Soho. Barrington tested the child's powers in various ways. He put before him the score of a duet with string accompaniment and asked him to play it at the keyboard and sing the upper part, Leopold taking the lower. He also suggested to the boy emotive ideas such as 'Love Song' and 'Song of Rage' which induced him to extemporise, at the harpsichord, two short recitatives and 'arias'. Wolfgang also modulated at a keyboard covered by a cloth, and wrote a bass to a previously unseen treble. Barrington wrote a long, fascinating account of his investigation, but – rather oddly – did nothing with it for nearly four years. In 1769 he addressed a report, according to the convention of the day, in the form of a letter to Dr. Mathew Maty, one of the two secretaries of the Royal Society. (The report was read on 15 February 1770, and published in 1771 in the *Philosophical Transactions,* the Society's journal.)

Now Maty, at the time of the Mozarts' visit, was also an under-librarian at the British Museum and secretary to its Trustees. It might be reasonable to suppose that it was his acquaintance with Barrington which served to bring the Mozarts to the Museum's notice. But he, like all the other staff then in post, had no knowledge of music or interest in it as a part of the collections. The same applied to the Trustees, at least until the appointment of James Harris (fig.2) on 3 May 1765. Harris, the father of the first Earl of Malmesbury, was a competent connoisseur of music, something of an expert in the composition of catches, and had been a friend of Handel. But we do not know if he ever met the Mozarts. One of the Trustees who did was the Rev. Dr. Thomas Birch (fig.3), Fellow of both the Royal Society and of the Society of Antiquaries, and a Trustee of the Museum since 1753. In his last letter from London, written on 9 July 1765, Leopold said that some days before, when he was dining with Count von Brühl, the Saxon ambassador, there was a huge fire in which Dr. Birch, 'our very good friend', lost some horses and the carriages in his stables. (Presumably the fire affected an area just south of the Strand, including Norfolk Street, where, as Leopold recorded in his diary, Birch lived.) Although there is no evidence in Birch's printed works and in published papers that he was at all musical, he lived in the same small world of learning as did Barrington, Maty, and Harris. Here, somewhere in this circle of scholarly men, must be the link between the Mozarts and the Museum.

It is important to establish this, because the gift which the Mozarts made was not offered by them spontaneously, but was solicited by the Trustees (let us suppose at the instance of Harris, perhaps prompted in the first place by Barrington). We know this from an anonymous newspaper report written in German and sent from London to Salzburg on 5 July 1765. This, if not the actual work of Leopold, was probably inspired by him, and it mentions the gift in some detail. The sequence of events cannot be dated precisely. Barrington did not state the date in June when he went to the Mozarts' lodging, and neither Leopold nor Nannerl dated the entries in their respective travel diaries, though it is clear from the context that each was writing towards the end of their stay in London.

Leopold's entry (in translation) simply reads: 'The Rev. Mr. Planta and his family in the British Museum'. Nannerl was concerned to record some

2. James Harris (1709–1780).
Stipple by Francesco Bartolozzi.
200 × 132mm.

JAMES HARRIS
MDCCLXXVI

of the wonders they had seen in and around London. After mentioning that she had noticed, in an unnamed park, a young elephant and a 'donkey with coffee-coloured stripes so natural that they could not have been painted better' – (? a zebra) – she proceeds to a breathless string of names: Westminster Abbey, Vauxhall, Ranelagh, the Tower, Richmond, Kew Gardens, Fulham Bridge, Westminster Hall, Kensington and the royal gardens. Then she goes on: 'the British Museum in which I saw the library, the antiquities, birds of all kinds, fishes, insects, fruits', and many other curiosities of natural history and science. Taken together, these two diary entries require some amplification.

The British Museum which the Mozarts saw was established only twelve years before their visit. It occupied the whole of Montagu House, a splendid mansion facing on to Great Russell Street and situated exactly where the present Museum stands. This mansion had been built from 1686 onwards for Ralph, first Duke of Montagu, and was the second of its name (an earlier one, erected in 1675–80, having been destroyed by fire). As befitted a wealthy owner who had served as British Ambassador

3. The Rev. Dr. Thomas Birch (1705–1766). Mezzotint by John Faber junior after James Wills. 1741. 355 × 252mm.

in Paris to the Court of Louis XIV, the mansion was in the French style. It had been purchased in 1753 to house the three great collections acquired for the nation by Parliament: the manuscripts of Sir Robert Cotton (1570–1631) and of Robert Harley, Earl of Oxford (1661–1724); and the immense, unparalleled variety of treasures accumulated by Sir Hans Sloane, Bart. (1660–1753) – manuscripts, printed books, drawings, coins and medals, antiquities from Greece, Italy, Assyria and other lands, insects, fishes, birds, specimens of minerals, fossils, shells and a huge range of what were then called 'natural productions'. As can be seen in fig.4, Montagu House looked on to a large courtyard flanked by two wings which ran south to the boundary wall. All this stood more or less intact until the mid-1840s, after which it was gradually demolished as the front of the present neo-classical building, designed by Sir Robert Smirke, rose on the site.

Montagu House opened its doors to the public in 1759, on a very restricted basis. To obtain an admission ticket was then normally a very slow process, and young children were not admitted. Clearly, the Mozarts came as privileged visitors. Their host, the Rev. Andrew Planta, was a

4. South front and courtyard of Montagu House in London, the original home of the British Museum. 1754. Engraving, by Sutton Nicholls. 235 × 450mm.

5. 'The Hall and Stair Case. British Museum.' 1808. Aquatint by J. Bluck after Thomas Rowlandson and Augustus Charles Pugin. 334 × 270mm.

member of a distinguished Swiss family from the Engadine. In 1753 he was appointed pastor of the German reformed church in London, and entered the service of the Trustees in 1757. (His son, Joseph, followed him, and rose to hold the highest office in the Museum, that of Principal Librarian, from 1799 to 1827.) Though still a fairly junior member of the staff in 1765, it was presumably because he spoke German that Andrew Planta was chosen to entertain the Mozarts and show them something of the Museum. Fig.5 illustrates the entrance hall and staircase of Montagu House as the visitors saw them, and plate I the view south-west towards the west wing, where, in accordance with the statutes, Planta and other officers resided. (The door in the left of the picture was perhaps that through which the Mozarts entered to be welcomed by Planta.)

It is likely, but not certain, that they brought their gift with them. Leopold possibly paid another visit to the Museum by himself to present a copy of his son's sonatas op.III (K10–15), for this item is not mentioned in the German report referred to above. The copy of it in the British Library's general collection of printed music (pressmark:h.61(7)) undoubtedly formed part of the total gift. Besides this, it comprised copies of Wolfgang's sonatas op.I (K6,7) – fig.6 – and op.II (K8,9), both printed in Paris in 1763; a copy of the engraving made in Paris by J. B. Delafosse after a watercolour of the Mozart musical family by L. C. de Carmontelle; and

6. Titlepage of Mozart's sonatas for violin and piano. K6, 7. First edition. 1764. 235 × 320mm.

7. Mozart's *God is our Refuge*, partly in his hand, partly in his father's. 1765. 240 × 295mm.

the manuscript of a four-part vocal work, superscribed: 'Chorus by Mr. Wolfgang Mozart. 1765' (fig.7).

This manuscript is a most interesting document. The superscription is entirely written by Leopold, as are also the first two of the three braces. Wolfgang probably wrote the clefs, the key signatures, the names of the voices, and the tempo markings. All the notes are certainly in his hand, likewise the first line of the words, which are those of the revised version of Psalm 46, verse 1. For this, he probably took as an exemplar a copy written out by his father on a separate sheet. But at the end of the first line Wolfgang got into difficulties, as can be seen from the meandering bar-lines, which are due to his having misjudged the space needed for the underlay of the broken syllables. At this point Leopold took over, and wrote the words in a clear firm hand. There is also evidence for this sharing of the work in the different colours of the ink. Throughout the lower staves the ink is dark brown – evidence of firm, well-controlled writing. On the top stave it is noticeably lighter, revealing the much weaker, uncertain pressure of the boy's hand.

Leopold's participation should not be regarded as an attempt to deceive the Trustees. During the 1760s and in the early 1770s Leopold regularly assisted his son in various ways to write his manuscript scores. Their respective handwritings became superficially similar. (Only in the last twenty years or so have all the essential differences been analysed and the share of father and son in various manuscripts been distinguished.) In *God is our Refuge* what matters is the ingenuity of the part-writing: this was Mozart's first and only setting of an English text, and seems to have been offered to the Trustees as an example of his skill, displayed in the manner

8. Leopold Mozart, with his son Wolfgang and his daughter Nannerl. Engraved by Jean Baptiste Delafosse after Louis Carrogis de Carmontelle. 1764. 380 × 228mm.

of a catch. The usual description, 'motet', is misleading, for it implies that the little piece was intended for liturgical use, which it was not.

Something should also be said about the painting by Carmontelle and the engraving (fig.8) made after it. We know from Leopold's letters that the watercolour (plate II) was executed several times – at least three copies are extant – in Paris in November 1763 and that the print was prepared next spring, shortly before the family left for London. While only Delafosse's name appears as the engraver, Leopold tells us that another artist shared in the work. This was Christian von Mechel, a native of Basle who later won fame as an illustrator and as the man who arranged the royal galleries at Vienna along chronological lines in the early 1780s. (The Mozarts seem to have known him quite well, and had intended, when in Paris, to stay at his house in the Rue St. Honoré.) Leopold used copies of the print as publicity on this great journey, and sometimes sent them for distribution in advance of their arrival on a particular tour.

There is a curious point about the representations of Leopold himself in the print and the watercolour, for he is seen playing the violin standing up with his legs crossed – a casual, unnatural posture. Perhaps Carmontelle painted him thus for the sake of artistic effect, in what was, almost certainly, a second version. For there exists another painting, also by Carmontelle, which shows only Leopold and Wolfgang, without Nannerl singing in front of the harpsichord. In it Leopold stands firmly on both feet and the boy is seated not on a chair but a backless seat with his feet on a stool instead of dangling in the air. Here, moreover, he is painted realistically rather than as the doll-like figure of the second version. (In fact, Carmontelle painted the features of all three Mozarts in rather a stylised manner.)

The print also served as publicity for Leopold himself, his prominence in the design being an eloquent reminder of his distinction as teacher and theorist of the violin. For his *Versuch einer gründlichen Violinschule* ('Treatise on the fundamental Principles of Violin Playing'), first published at Augsburg in 1756, was already becoming widely known. A Dutch edition, with his portrait on the titlepage (fig.9), was to appear in 1766: French versions were issued later in about 1770 and again in about 1805. Besides all these, the British Library's collections include subsequent German editions of 1787 and 1800, another issued at Vienna in 1806, and a very rare English abridgment of *c*.1815. Among later printings are the first complete English edition of 1948 and a selected Hungarian edition, issued in 1965. The *Violinschule* became a standard work in its field, and would have given Leopold Mozart a secure place in musical history even if he had not been the father of a genius.

Considered as a whole, the Mozart gift is notable for several reasons. It included, as the record of the Museum's 'Book of Presents' shows, the first music ever given to the Trustees: moreover, it was then contemporary music. (The quantity of important music, manuscript and printed, in the foundation collections dates from much earlier periods.) This gift was the only one made by Mozart to any national institution, and the visit described above was a unique event in his life.

Although the family's visit to the British Museum took place at the time when Leopold Mozart was extremely busy with arrangements for their imminent departure, it must have made a lasting impression on him. For he carefully preserved the Trustees' formal acknowledgement (fig.10), which passed, much creased and folded, to his son, later to the latter's widow, and ultimately to the Mozarteum in Salzburg. (It is perhaps worth noting that the phrase 'musical performances' was used in the eighteenth century to mean 'compositions'.) The poor physical condition of the Museum also seems to have impressed Leopold, because four years later, in March 1770, he wrote to his wife from Bologna: 'We have been to the

9. Leopold Mozart.
Engraving by
Joannes Enschedé.
1766.
190 × 150mm.

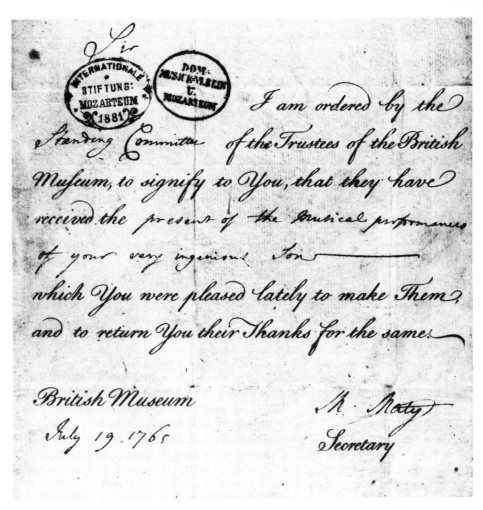

Sir

I am ordered by the Standing Committee of the Trustees of the British Museum, to signify to You, that they have received the present of the Musical performances of your very ingenious Son which You were pleased lately to make Them, and to return You their Thanks for the same.

British Museum
July 19. 1765

M. Maty
Secretary

10. Receipt given to Leopold Mozart, acknowledging the gift of his son's 'musical performances' to the British Museum. Engraved, with details added 19 July 1765 in the hand of Mathew Maty, secretary to the Trustees. 225 × 185mm.

Instituto [the 'Istituto di Scienze e Arti', in the Palazzo Poggi] and admired the fine statues of our Court Statuarius [Johann Baptist Hagenauer]. What I have seen in Bologna surpasses the British Museum. For here one can see not only the rarities of nature but everything else that deserves the name of science, preserved like a dictionary in fine rooms, in a clear and orderly fashion'. This unfavourable comparison was undeniably just. For when the Mozarts were at the Museum it already suffered from lack of space and staff: its display was overcrowded and unsystematic. Even fifteen years later a French visitor to London, Barthélémi de Saint Fond, wrote: 'With the exception of some fishes in a small apartment, which are begun to be classed, nothing is in order, and everything is out of its place'. Leopold might have been glad to know that his recollection was not inaccurate, and

Nannerl pleased that the fishes which attracted her attention were better cared for!

The Mozarts left London on 24 July 1765, only five days after Maty sent, or gave, the Trustees' acknowledgement to Leopold. After a short stay in or near Canterbury, where they went to the races, they made their way to Dover on 1 August and crossed the channel to Calais on the first stage of their long, devious journey home. None of them ever returned to England, although Mozart himself nearly did so on more than one occasion.

In the late autumn of 1786 he and his wife were planning to go to London for some considerable time, apparently at the suggestion of their English friends who were then all leaving Vienna – Thomas Attwood, Michael Kelly (the first Don Basilio), the composer Stephen Storace and his sister Nancy (the first Susanna). But this came to nothing because Leopold, then sixty-seven, refused to look after little Karl, the Mozarts' two-year-old son. Two actual invitations came in 1790. On 26 October Robert May O'Reilly, the manager of an Italian opera company at the Pantheon in Oxford Street, wrote to Mozart with a clear proposal. He said that 'through a person attached to H.R.H. the Prince of Wales', he had heard of Mozart's intention – based, one imagines, on rumours in German newspapers – to come to London. He offered him £300 to compose at least two operas between December 1790 and the end of June 1791, with the additional opportunity of writing for the professional concerts. Mozart's reply has not survived.

The second invitation came in December. J. P. Salomon, the London impresario, had been travelling in Europe to engage artists for his next season, and reached Vienna in the hope of inducing Haydn to return to England with him. Salomon succeeded in this, but failed to persuade Mozart to follow later. Had any of these plans or possibilities become a reality, and had Mozart, with or without his wife, retraced the steps of his childhood in London, it is likely that he would have visited the British Museum again. Might he not then have enriched it with a new manuscript, to be added to the earlier gift? Yet though this was not to be, the Museum's contact with the Mozart family, however indirect and long-delayed, was not to be entirely lost.

2. Vincent Novello and the Mozart Family

During the latter part of the eighteenth century and the early decades of the nineteenth, the British Museum's collections of music grew very slowly. Printed works were acquired almost entirely by copyright deposit, the source of a few important Mozart editions which will be mentioned later. In general the Museum had at this time no plan at all for the systematic acquisition of music, whether printed or manuscript, by composers who were contemporary or nearly so. (In this respect, it was no different from the Bodleian Library or any other comparable collection. Apart from the interest of enthusiastic amateurs, music was generally considered to be for performance, not for collecting and study.) Consequently, donation remained an invaluable source of enrichment.

After the events described in the preceding chapter, nearly eighty years elapsed before any more Mozart manuscripts were added to the Museum's collections. When this happened, in 1843, it was as a gift from Vincent Novello (1781–1861), founder of the famous firm of music publishers and one of the most influential and public-spirited musicians of his generation (fig.11). Not only had he long revered the memory of Mozart, to him 'the Shakespeare of music', but he was much concerned at the unsatisfactory state of the musical collections in the British Museum. These two things may seem unrelated. But they were linked in Novello's tenacious mind, and together led to the renewal of an English connection with the Mozart family and ultimately to his very generous musical gift (one of many) to the Museum.

On 24 May 1824 Novello wrote a long letter to Henry Bankes, M.P. for Corfe Castle, and a Trustee of the British Museum, about the music in that institution. He drew attention to the total lack of an acquisitions policy (particularly for manuscripts), to the absence of any staff with specialised knowledge, and urged the need for proper catalogues. Novello also pointed out the ineffectiveness of deposit as required by the Copyright Act, and concluded by modestly offering his own services. His proposals never seem to have been laid before the Trustees formally. During the next sixteen years protests against the Museum's neglect of music were made in the press and in the form of memoranda submitted by other musicians to the Trustees. When at last they took action, in 1840, it was along the very lines which Novello, as scholar, editor and practical musician, had suggested to Bankes.

After 1824, Novello continued to work in many fields of music. Then, late in 1828 or early in 1829, news reached London which caused him to translate his veneration for Mozart into practical action. It was apparently J. A. Stumpff (fig.12), a harp maker resident in London, formerly a friend of Beethoven, and later a collector of Mozart autographs, who heard that Mozart's sister lay sadly and seriously ill in Salzburg. The brilliant little girl who, as 'Nannerl', had shared the triumphs of Mozart's childhood, had become by her marriage in 1784 Freifrau Hofrath Maria Anna von Berchtold zu Sonnenburg. Now, long-widowed and in her seventy-eighth year, she was blind, half-paralysed and bedridden. Novello proposed to a number of his fellow musicians in London that they should subscribe to a gift of money to alleviate her distress. The contributors numbered seventeen and included, besides Novello himself, Stumpff, and Thomas Attwood, who had once been Mozart's pupil: the total raised was £63. They decided to entrust to Novello the task of conveying the money personally to the old lady. So on 24 June 1829 he and his wife, Mary Sabilla, set out for Salzburg; and each kept an independent diary of their travels, in which they recorded not only what they saw but also their conversations with the people they met.

11. Vincent Novello
(1781–1861).
Unsigned engraving.
124 × 100mm.

12. Johann Andreas
Stumpff
(1769–1846).
Unsigned woodcut.
150 × 120mm.

13. Constanze
(Mozart) Nissen
(1762–1842).
Miniature by
Thomas Spitzer.
1826.
66 × 59mm.

14. Figured bass progressions in the autograph of Leopold Mozart, K626b/39, once thought to be in his son's hand. 130 × 280mm.

15. Mozart's concert rondo for soprano, *Al desio, di chi t'adora*, K577. 1789. Copy by Laurent Lausch. Part of the final leaf with an autograph cadenza added by Mozart. 115 × 305mm.

Such was the immediate purpose of Vincent Novello's journey. It enabled him also to use his visit to Salzburg (and its extension to Vienna, which lies beyond the scope of this book) to fulfil a plan that had been maturing in his mind for some time – to travel to Austria to seek out Mozart's surviving relatives and friends in order to collect information from them for use in a biography of the composer. In Salzburg (plate III), besides visiting Mozart's sister, the Novellos met his former wife Constanze (fig.13), now widowed again by the death of her second husband, Georg Nikolaus Nissen (see fig.38) in 1826. During the three days, 14 to 17 July, which they spent in her company, they quickly formed a tie of quite extraordinary intimacy, which they renewed on 3 August, during their return journey from Vienna. It was on the latter occasion that 'Madame Nissen', as the Novellos called her, gave Vincent some manuscripts as a keepsake.

Only one of them is entirely in Mozart's hand. This is a narrow strip, clearly cut from a larger sheet, containing a keyboard version of the minuet no.3 and the trio no.6 of a set of sixteen dances for small orchestra, K176, which he composed in 1773. (The date of this arrangement is unknown.) At the foredge is a note: 'the hand-writing of Mozart, given by the composer's widow to Vincent Novello, and by him presented to the Musical Library of the British Museum.'

The next is a small oblong octavo sheet (fig.14) containing a contrapuntal exercise in four parts. Beneath the music is a note by Constanze: 'Scritura di Mio Marito Mozart per il mio carissimo amico Novello Salisburgo il 3 augusto [sic] 1829'. In the margin Novello wrote: 'A beautiful specimen of Mozart's handwriting kindly given me when I had the gratification of visiting her and Mozart's younger son Wolfgang, at Salzburg, in the year 1829'. It has been established that this sheet is entirely in Leopold Mozart's handwriting. As mentioned in the previous chapter, there was a superficial resemblance between his hand and his son's, but in the early nineteenth century the real differences had not been observed.

The third manuscript provides a rare glimpse of the very close musical affinity between Mozart and Constanze. It is a copy, in vocal score, made by the Viennese copyist Laurent Lausch, of the rondo for soprano 'Al desio, di chi t'adora' (K577) preceded by the recitative from Le nozze di Figaro, 'Giunse il fin al momento'. Constanze wrote on the verso of the manuscript a dedication to Novello, who added the following: 'This manuscript is the identical copy from which Mozart used to accompany his wife when she sang this beautiful composition. He also wrote a little cadenza for her, which is still to be found in his own handwriting at the end of the song'. This is illustrated in fig.15.

Constanze's fourth gift to Novello was an autograph score, not by Mozart but by his younger son Franz Xaver Wolfgang, usually known as Wolfgang Amadeus the younger. Its titlepage reads: 'Wolfgang Amadeus

31

Mozart junior. Aria buffo. . . Composta per il suo caro carissimo padre G. N. Nissen. Opera 13. Wien 15 Januar 1808'. Below this Constanze wrote: 'à mon ami Novello de Constanza [sic] Nissen veuve Mozart le 3 august Salzburg 1829'. Novello's annotation explains why the younger Mozart wrote the piece when barely seventeen and a half years old: 'On the birth-day of Mozart's widow, it was customary for the family to get up one of Mozart's operas privately amongst themselves as their principal amusement for the evening. At one of these domestic performances, the opera of *Il direttore della commedia* [*Der Schauspieldirektor*] was chosen and Mozart's son Wolfgang (who was then about 18 years of age) composed an "Aria Buffo" expressly for the occasion at the request of his father-in-law Mr. Nissen to whom he was much attached. This is the identical score in his own handwriting and which was very kindly presented to me by his mother when I had the gratification of visiting her in 1829'. On the verso of the last leaf Stumpff wrote an English verse translation of the text on 7 October 1830, 'for and with kind compliments to Mr. Novello'.

Besides giving us a charming glimpse of Constanze's domestic life, the two original inscriptions point to a curious relationship between the younger Mozart and Nissen. The latter had in fact been very good to Mozart's sons and supervised their education. But in 1808 Nissen was not their 'padre', as the dedication of this aria puts it. He and Constanze had been living together for several years, and did not marry until 1809. Perhaps Novello was hinting at this irregularity by his use of the words 'father-in-law'. His diary shows that he was delighted to have met Mozart's son, who quite by chance had come to Salzburg at the time of the Novellos' visit. It was he who escorted them to their rather sad meeting with his aunt, and he too who unwittingly illustrated how remarkably attached his mother became to the Novellos, especially to Vincent. For during a walk they took together on 3 August she poured into Vincent's sympathetic ear her concern at her son's prolonged liaison with a married countess in Poland (where he was employed). Constanze feared that this would prevent him settling in Vienna, where his gifts would be better recognised. Seldom can a friendship have ripened so quickly as that between Constanze Nissen and Vincent Novello.

Such were the four Mozart documents which Novello brought back with him from his travels. Within barely two years, another, entirely in the composer's hand, came his way. This was the autograph of the duet sonata in B flat major, K358, written in 1774. The fluency of Mozart's hand (fig.16) seems to reflect the spontaneity of this delightful work. The autograph bears a German inscription written by Mozart's sister: 'Dass diese Composition von meinem Bruder componiert und geschrieben ist, bezeugnet seine Schwester Maria Anna Freifrau von Berchtold zu Sonnenburg'. ('I, Baroness Maria Anna Berchtold zu Sonnenberg, Mozart's sister, testify that this work is composed and written by my

16. Mozart's Duet sonata in B flat major, K358/186c. Autograph. Primo part of the opening of the third movement. 230 × 315mm.

brother'.) Presumably she had retained the autograph as having been Mozart's duet partner. Another, rather tantalising, inscription reads: 'From Mozart's sister to Winslow Young, Esqre, from Winslow Young to his brother Charles Young, from Charles Young to Miss May Tomkison (now Mrs. Fouché), and from Mrs. Fouché to Lydia B. Hunt, from Lydia Hunt to her highly respected friend Vincent Novello, 1832'. When Winslow Young visited Mozart's sister is not known, but her clear, firm handwriting suggests that it was while her eyesight was unimpaired.

During his visit to Vienna Novello acquired a Beethoven sketch leaf, and later on the autograph of a 3-part organ fugue by Mendelssohn, dated 29 March 1833. He treasured all these manuscripts until 1843, when on 27 July he gave them, together with the four keepsakes of Constanze Mozart and the duet sonata, to the British Museum, where they now form MS 14193 in the Additional series. When Novello made this extraordinarily generous gift, he had not perhaps entirely forgotten that, nearly twenty years before, he sought to draw attention to the defects of the 'Musical

Library'. Indeed, in 1832 he had some personal experience of them. We know that in 1828 he bought one of the first copies of Nissen's voluminous biography of Mozart to reach England. After returning from Salzburg, Novello must have read it right through – it lacks an index – and found the passage which describes the gift of 'the 4-part chorus' to the British Museum. In 1832 he went to the Museum, and asked to see the manuscript. As there was still no music catalogue of any kind, and as Nissen had not cited the English words, this seems to have been an awkward enquiry. But in the end the sheet was produced for him, and Novello made a copy of it. In a note added to his titlepage, he revealed that the original had been found 'after a very long search', and further commented: 'It is remarkable (&, in my opinion, a very reprehensible neglect) that Mozart's name does not once appear in any of the Museum's catalogues'. Perhaps his gift of 1843 was encouraged by the publication in 1842 of a catalogue of the music manuscripts, including *God is our Refuge*. Novello's copy of it came to light in 1981, and was acquired by the British Library as another token of his devotion to Mozart.

3. The Chamber Music Autographs

(i) The 'ten quartets'

Quite early in his adult life, Mozart acquired the habit – perhaps inculcated by Leopold – of preserving his autographs. A few he gave away, and a number were lost, but at his death the collection was a large one, and most of it was unpublished. It passed to Constanze, who became aware of its value early in 1799 when she received a request for information about it from Breitkopf & Härtel, the famous Leipzig music publishers. When she ultimately proposed that they should buy the entire collection, they hesitated, and took only some forty autographs, leaving her with the rest. At this point, Constanze received an offer from Johann Anton André, a music publisher in Offenbach am Main. She accepted it in September 1799, and he paid her 3150 gulden (about £320) for the collection which ultimately amounted to 280 items. André treasured this collection and published from it quite a number of works for the first time. As he grew older, he became worried about its fate. A year or so before his death in 1842, he offered it successively to the courts of Vienna, Berlin and London, but all refused. Had the negotiations with London (conducted through Novello's friend J. A. Stumpff – see fig.12 – and his son Gustav) been successful, this collection would presumably have become part of the Royal Music Library which, deposited on loan in the British Museum in 1911, was presented outright to it in 1957.

It is against this background that we can now turn to that small part of André's collection which fortunately found its way to England, some twelve years after his purchase from Constanze. While we know that André gave away an autograph now and again to a friend, we do not know how in 1811 (or, as another account has it, in 1814) Stumpff persuaded him to sell twenty-two autographs, comprising chamber music and various keyboard works, for £150. Stumpff seems to have made the purchase as an investment, for in about 1815 he tried – apparently by raffle – to sell the manuscripts, which Attwood duly authenticated. But this failed, and Stumpff kept his treasures, inscribing his name on the first leaf of many of them. (It is recorded that early in 1843 he gave a private quartet party at which the autographs were used for performance, and Mozart's health was drunk at 4 a.m.) In about 1845 Stumpff made another attempt to sell them, again by raffle, but this too came to nothing and the collection was sold by auction soon after his death in November 1846. Whatever his original motive for the purchase, he certainly combined judgment with powers of persuasion. For the autographs which André parted with included the six string quartets dedicated to Haydn, the 'Hoffmeister' quartet in D major, K499, and the last three quartets which Mozart wrote for the King of Prussia. There were also the string quintets in D major and E flat major, the great violin sonata in B flat major, K454, the fantasia and sonata for piano in C minor, K475, K457, and the adagio in B minor, K540.

The jewel of this collection was undoubtedly the 'ten string quartets' as they are often called, and it is these which came to the British Museum in 1907. At the sale of Stumpff's effects on 30 March 1847, Mr. Charles H. Chichele Plowden paid £5.15.0 for the 'Haydn' quartets, and £3.3.0 for the 'Hoffmeister'. A music dealer named C. J. Hamilton bought the 'Prussian' quartets for £4.6.0, and sold them to Plowden on the day after the sale. Plowden, an amateur of music, was a Fellow of the Royal Geographical Society and Fellow of the Society of Antiquaries. At his death in 1866 those Mozart autographs passed to his daughter Harriet, who lived in Chislehurst, and she, persuaded, it seems, by Barclay Squire, bequeathed them to the British Museum in 1907. But that was not quite the end of the story. Hearing from Squire of the bequest, Edward Speyer, a wealthy patron of music, wrote an enthusiastic letter to *The Times,* praising Miss Plowden's generosity, and pointing out that the value of the bequest was at least £6000. Thereupon, her heirs took legal action against the Museum, but the Trustees' right to the bequest was upheld in the courts. Such, in the event, was the curious path by which a unique group of Mozart's finest chamber music in autograph passed from André's purchase to the Museum.

In this group, the six quartets which Mozart (fig.17) dedicated to Haydn (fig.18) are of outstanding interest. The first of them, the G major, K387, bears the date 31 December 1782 in Mozart's hand: the last, the C major, K465, he entered in his thematic catalogue (see p.53–6) on 14 January 1785. The six works thus occupied him during two of the busiest years of his life, during which he composed much else, including six masterly piano concertos, concertos for horn, parts of the C minor Mass, and some fine works for various chamber groups.

From a pioneering study of the music-paper which Mozart used, Alan Tyson has been able to show that he did not write the six quartets, as has usually been said, in two fairly continuous groups of three, separated by some lapse of time. In fact, he would start one of them, put it on one side, and return to it later; he worked on different sections of two quartets at the same time. Tyson also shows that the 'Hunt' quartet, in B flat, caused Mozart such difficulty, involving several false starts, that it occupied him intermittently for over a year. While the autograph of the D minor quartet, K421, reveals no such secrets, it lacks a date, which can, however, be

17. Mozart.
Engraved, 1789, by
Johann Georg
Mansfeld after a
plaster medallion by
Leonard Posch.
168 × 110mm.

18. Franz Joseph
Haydn
(1732–1809).
Engraving by
Johann Ernst
Mansfeld. 1781.
160 × 110mm.

supplied from later evidence. Constanze Mozart let it be known in a magazine article printed in 1799 that her husband was composing this work on 17 June 1783, sitting in a room adjacent to that in which she was giving birth to their first son, Raimund Leopold. Talking to the Novellos in 1829, she confirmed this, and added that the minuet reflected Mozart's reaction to her distress.

The distinctive musical quality of these quartets is reflected in the dedication to Haydn, in which Mozart said that they were 'il frutto di una lunga, e laboriosa fatica' ('the fruit of a sustained, laborious effort'). Mozart refers here to the challenge which Haydn's quartets, op.33, had posed him. In the preface to the first edition, dated 3 December 1781, Haydn had emphasised 'the new and special way' in which they were composed. By this he meant that he could now give all four instruments an equal share in the musical discourse. Mozart now had to face the difficulty of expanding and refining this innovation, which he did by learning to develop his musical thought without apparent effort in four parts at will.

19. Titlepage of Mozart's six quartets dedicated to Haydn. First edition. 1785. 334 × 235mm.

Ansicht vom Graben gegen den Kohlmarkt. Vue du Graben vers le Kohlmarkt.

20. View of the Graben in Vienna, looking towards the Kohlmarkt. Mozart lived in the Graben from 1781–82, and again for most of 1784. Engraving by Karl Schütz, coloured by hand. 1781. 350 × 460mm.

But Tyson's research has corroborated Mozart's statement about the difficulty he had in achieving this. The completed set is perhaps the most important group of any of his works published in his lifetime, and on no other titlepage (see fig.19) did he express his feelings as warmly as he did here in the words 'dal suo amico' – this to a composer twenty-three years his senior, and by far the greatest of his contemporaries.

The publisher matched the importance of the music with a splendid titlepage, boldly designed, finely proportioned and diversified with an elegant variety of lettering (fig.19). The two composers had first met in Vienna (fig.20) in December 1781: their mutual regard quickly ripened, and lasted until Mozart's death. Michael Kelly mentions a quartet party in 1784 at which Haydn took the first violin part and Mozart the viola. We may be fairly sure that there were other similar occasions. Indeed, Leopold Mozart, writing to his daughter early in 1785, mentions two of them. On 22 January, reporting a short letter received from his son, he wrote from Salzburg: 'He adds that last Saturday he performed his six quartets for his friend Haydn'. Again, after travelling to Vienna, he wrote on 16 February, about a performance of the last three in the presence of the dedicatee: 'Haydn said to me: "Before God and as an honest man, I tell you that your son is the greatest composer known to me either in person or by name. He

21. Mozart's String quartet in C major, K465.
Autograph.
Opening of the first movement.
230 × 320mm.

has taste and, what is more, the most profound knowledge of composition"'. This oft-quoted remark never loses its ringing sincerity: it is surely one of the most generous tributes ever paid by one musical genius to another. The autographs and the first edition are the visible form of the special type of music which forged the bond between Haydn and Mozart.

The autographs also show a point of particular interest in their relation to the Artaria edition. Generally, it is the autograph and not the first edition which is considered to provide the most accurate text. But for the 'Haydn' quartets comparison reveals that the engraved parts differ from what Mozart wrote in so many important details, such as tempo indications, dynamic markings, and phrasing, that in such cases the reading of the first edition is definitive. (For instance, the autograph of the trio of the A major quartet does not contain a single expression mark, but over twenty were inserted in the first edition.) The nature and extent of these changes make it likely, to put it no higher, that Mozart read the proofs and made them himself. (At the least he would have authorised them to be made by his pupil Josephine Auernhammer, who is known to have done such work on some of his piano pieces.)

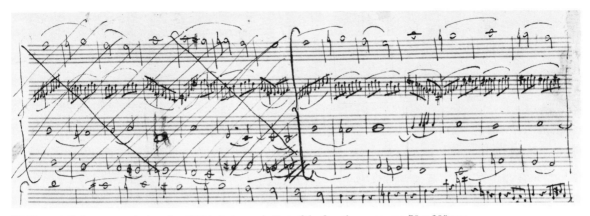

22. Mozart's String quartet in A major, K464. Autograph. Part of the fourth movement. 78 × 305mm.

23. Mozart's String quartet in G major, K387. Autograph. Opening of the third movement, with the composer's directions to the copyist in the margin. 230 × 315mm.

In the scores of these quartets Mozart's handwriting is generally neat and precise, even in the most difficult passages. We should not suppose, however, that he wrote them all down straight out of his head. The survival of sketches for a variety of works dating from his later years makes it likely that he made them, for example, for the complex harmonic progressions in the slow introduction to the first movement of K465 (fig.21), where the only uncertainties are a slight smudge and one alteration. We know that a number of scholars examined this autograph, while it was owned successively by Plowden and his daughter, to verify that the harsh dissonances of these twenty-two bars, as printed in the current editions, were really what Mozart wrote. Elsewhere, for instance in the first and last movements of the A major quartet, K464, cancellations show how he could change his mind when in the full flow of creative writing (fig.22). An example of the delicacy of Mozart's handwriting is shown in fig.23, which reproduces the opening of the Andante cantabile of the G major quartet K387, where his placing of the very small notes of the gruppetti is unmistakably clear and precise. In the margin of this leaf we can also see that Mozart wrote some directions to the copyist who apparently visited his home to prepare the parts: 'Izt wird nur von diessem Andante das 2te Violin und die Viola herausgeschrieben'. 'Die Bass Stimme Kommt erst nach Tisch'. 'Das erste Violin ist schon geschrieben'. ('At present, only the second violin and the viola parts of this Andante are to be copied out. The

bass part is to be done after dinner. The first violin is already written out'.)
Such instructions are very rarely found in Mozart's scores.

He entered the quartet in D major, K499, in his thematic catalogue on 19
August 1786. It has become known as the 'Hoffmeister' quartet, after the
name of F. A. Hoffmeister, the Viennese publisher who issued the first
edition, to distinguish it from other Mozart quartets in the same key. This
work poses a question. During that summer, after the success of *Le nozze di
Figaro,* in barely ten weeks – from 3 June to early August – he had written
seven important works for chamber groups or for keyboard, and a horn
concerto. Why did he then add to his burden by composing this solitary
quartet, the medium which caused him most difficulty? Unless, perhaps, it
was to repay a debt to Hoffmeister, there is no answer to this question. But,
although the autograph reveals no secrets of chronology, we may be
certain, from the evidence of the last three quartets, that the difficulties
were still there in 1786.

It was probably during the spring of 1789, when Mozart was on a visit to
Berlin (fig.24), that he received a commission from Frederick William II,
the King of Prussia, who was an enthusiastic cellist, to compose six string
quartets. The three which Mozart (fig.25) ultimately finished – his last –

25. Mozart. Photogravure of
the silver point drawn at
Dresden by Doris Stock,
March or April 1789.
175 × 135mm.

thus became known as the 'Prussian' quartets and their autographs complete the group of ten which was sold by André to Stumpff and is now in the British Library. Mozart wrote the first of the three, K575 in D major, fairly quickly, and entered it in his catalogue in June, 'for His Majesty the King of Prussia'. In this work, especially in the first movement, the cello part is given remarkable prominence, no doubt to please the royal player. But the consequent imbalance seems to have given Mozart some trouble, as can be seen for example in the very first page of the autograph (fig.26). Here he twice crossed out the parts for viola and cello, and inverted them, using the bass stave for the viola and *vice versa,* in order to accommodate the cello's highest register.

When Mozart completed the other two quartets, K589 in B flat major, and K590 in F major, in the summer of 1790, he referred to the task (in a letter of 12 June) as 'diese mühsame Arbeit' ('this troublesome labour'). Besides corroborating these words with corrections and cancellations, these three autographs contain other evidence of a more subtle kind. From an intricate, highly illuminating study of the paper-types used in the

26. Mozart's String quartet in D major, K575.
Autograph.
Opening of the first movement.
238 × 315mm.

autographs of the three quartets, Alan Tyson has demonstrated that Mozart was telling the simple truth. For all the 'Haydn' quartets and for K499 he used twelve-stave paper. But for the whole of K575 and part of K589, he used ten-stave paper which, as Tyson deduced from the watermarks, he could only have bought in Dresden or Prague, on his way back from Berlin to Vienna. (This ten-stave paper was wasteful for quartets because two staves on each page were useless.) After beginning the commission during his journey, on the ten-stave paper, Mozart had to put it aside to work on *Così fan tutte*. When he came back to the quartets in May and June 1790, he reverted to his more economical twelve-stave paper for the last two movements of K589 and the whole of K590. This paper, as it happened, was of several distinctive types, and from their distribution in the autographs it seems clear that Mozart worked on the two last quartets simultaneously and rather unsystematically before he entered them in his catalogue, doubtless with a feeling of relief that 'this troublesome labour', at least, was behind him.

(ii) Various chamber works

Thanks to the fortunate chances which kept together the autographs of the quartets, they form a coherent group unique for the study of Mozart's development as a composer of chamber music. We can now pass on to the other single manuscripts in this category, in all six complete works and some most interesting drafts and fragments. Some are in the British Library's own collections, while others form part of two deposited on loan. They date at intervals from Mozart's teens to the last year of his life, and show something of the extraordinary range of his genius in this field.

In August and September 1773 Mozart was in Vienna, and there completed six string quartets, three of which, in part or whole, claim our attention here. For the first, K168 in F major, he composed what is probably an earlier version of the minuet, K168a, on one side of a leaf, the other side of which he used to write out cadenzas to two piano concertos by contemporary composers, Ignaz von Beecke and Leontzi Honauer. (See p.50 below.) This leaf remained in Constanze Mozart's possession after she sold the bulk of her husband's autographs to André. In 1835, in order to give a present to someone who had helped her, she cut the leaf into two unequal parts, the smaller of which bore the cadenza for Honauer's concerto and on its reverse the viola and cello part only of the last sixteen bars of the minuet. (Fortunately the larger strip comprising the other cadenza and the rest of the minuet survives, in an American collection.) The smaller strip came to the British Museum in 1953 as part of the bequest of E. H. W. Meyerstein, who had formerly been a member of the staff of the Department of Manuscripts.

The autograph of the fifth of Mozart's 1773 quartets, K172 in B flat major, ultimately passed to the notable English collector Julian Marshall, and was bought from him (with many autographs by other composers) by the British Museum on 26 March 1881. At its head are the words 'Quartetto V' in Mozart's hand. (He had stated, rather unusually, at the head of K168 that this was the first of a set of six.) The whole score is written with remarkable clarity: only on fol.7 recto is there a substantial correction – one bar deleted and rewritten in the lower left hand margin. If we remember how difficult Mozart found the composition of the 'Haydn' quartets, it is almost inconceivable that, nearly nine years earlier, he could have written K172 straight out of his head. This autograph looks very much like a fair copy. That Mozart did make drafts at this time is exemplified in the case of the sixth quartet, K173, in D minor, for which he decided to compose the finale in fugal style, on a long descending chromatic subject. There is an earlier version of this movement running to eighty-three bars written on three leaves, and showing considerable differences from the final text. This draft is one of the pieces in the Mozart collection which was formed by Stefan Zweig (1881–1942) and deposited on loan by his heirs in the British Museum in 1957.

Another important autograph draft relates to the piano quartet in E flat major, K493. This leaf, which forms part of the Wandering Minstrels' archive in the Music Library, bears the second version (the first is found on another sketch leaf, in a private English collection) for the flowing opening melody of the third movement of this quartet. It provides a good example of the trouble Mozart could take to refine his melodic ideas.

The autograph of the string quintet in C minor, K406, is another of those which were formerly the property of J. A. Stumpff, after whose death it ultimately passed to Julian Marshall, who sold it to the Museum at the same time as the quartet in B flat major, K172. This quintet is a skilful and revealing arrangement, made by Mozart himself, of his wind serenade, K388, and probably dates from the spring of 1787, the time when he composed the string quintets in C major and G minor. Mozart seems to have produced the quintet in C minor with a view to increasing the number of his works available in this form. We know that in 1788 he was advertising for sale (without, it seems, much success) manuscript copies of all three quintets.

The string quintet in E flat major, K614, Mozart's last work in this form, was completed on 12 April 1791. This autograph, like that of K406, was once in Stumpff's possession, and now forms part of the Stefan Zweig collection. It is written with marvellous clarity, even in the most complex contrapuntal passages. After the last bars of the finale, Mozart wrote out the title of the work, in the manner of a colophon, on six lines thus: Quintetto | a 2 violini | 2 viole | e | violoncello | di Wolfgango Amadeo Mozart |. Only two other autographs of his have a similar subscription.

Another Zweig autograph is that of a quintet for armonica, flute, oboe, viola and cello, K617, which opens with an adagio in C minor, leading to an allegretto in the major. Mozart completed the autograph on 23 May 1791: he composed the work for Marianne Kirchgessner, the then famous blind virtuoso on the armonica, a strange instrument which needs, perhaps, a brief description. Derived from the far older 'musical glasses', the armonica consisted of a three-octave range of glass bowls, 'nested' as *The New Grove Dictionary of Music* says, 'within one another concentrically on a horizontal axle which is turned with a pedal'. The rims of the revolving bowls, well moistened before use, were touched by the player's finger tips. Some models were fitted with a shallow tray of water, so that the rims of most of the glasses were kept moist automatically as they revolved. Mozart had long known the distinctive ethereal sound of this instrument, for Leopold Mozart, in a letter written from Vienna in August 1773, mentions that his son played it at that time. (Leopold also said that he longed to have an armonica himself.) In the actual score of K617 Mozart uses for the instrument what seems to be a French term, 'harmonique', though in his thematic catalogue he wrote 'harmonica' (not to be confused with 'harmonika', the modern German term for the mouth-organ).

The last Zweig autograph of a chamber work is the violin sonata in F major, K377, which was once the property of A. G. Kurtz, a collector in Wavertree, near Liverpool, who acquired it at an anonymous Sotheby sale. One interesting feature of this autograph is that it includes seventeen cancelled bars of a false start which Mozart made to the slow movement.

4. Other Mozart Works in Autograph

(i) Instrumental

The Stefan Zweig collection contains three autographs of instrumental music. The earliest is the first of three marches for orchestra, K408 in C major, which Mozart composed for an unknown occasion, probably in 1782. It seems also to have been a favourite in the Mozart household, for he made a piano arrangement of the piece, and in 1799 Constanze told Breitkopf & Härtel that he had done it for her. The horn concerto, in E flat major, K447, is one of Mozart's several masterpieces for this instrument, and dates probably from the early months of 1783. Like the other concerted pieces and the quintet for horn and strings, K447 was written for his Viennese friend Ignaz Leutgeb, a marvellous player on this difficult instrument which, at that time, had no valves. In the autograph of K447 Mozart wrote in his friend's name twice, in the form 'Leitgeb' and each time after a pause (fig.27), indicating perhaps that he should extemporise a cadenza. The second movement, marked 'larghetto', is headed 'Romance di Wolfgango Amadeo Mozart', an unusual superscription at this point in a three-movement work, which suggests that this and the concluding Allegro might have been composed at a different time from the first movement. The third Zweig autograph is the undated score of a set of five dances, K609, which Mozart probably wrote in 1791. (He failed to enter it in his thematic catalogue.) During his last years in Vienna, he composed half a dozen similar sets, all for court balls. The first of the five dances in K609 is particularly interesting because he used for its opening (fig.28) the same widely popular air 'Non più andrai' from his own opera, *Le nozze di Figaro*, which he had already quoted in the finale of Act II of *Don Giovanni*.

The British Library's own collections have only one Mozart work in concerto form, and an incomplete one at that. But its very incompleteness makes it of unusual interest. This work is the rondo in A major for piano and orchestra, K386, which the composer dated 19 October 1782. The unpublished autograph had remained in J. A. André's possession and, together with some more of Mozart's and others of J. S. Bach, Haydn and Weber, was brought to London early in 1838 by André's son Gustav, so that they could all be offered for sale. At this time the London publisher Charles Coventry, a close friend of the composer Sterndale Bennett, was bringing out a large collection of Mozart's piano music in an edition prepared by Cipriani Potter. The latter was given access to the autograph

27. Mozart's Horn concerto in E flat major, K447. Autograph. Part of the third movement, showing a pause for a cadenza with the surname of the soloist, Ignaz Leutgeb, written by the composer above this point. 111 × 309mm.

28. Mozart's Five contredances for orchestra, K609. Autograph. Opening of no.1 in which Mozart introduced the melody 'Non più andrai' from *Le nozze di Figaro*. 75 × 180mm.

of this Rondo in A, which he arranged for piano solo, so producing the first edition for inclusion in Coventry's collection. But as the autograph lacked the last two bifolia, Potter supplied the ending himself.

Within the next few years Bennett seems to have acquired the autograph, and by 1846, or even earlier, began to give away pieces to friends, retaining for himself in the end only three leaves and a fragment. The last two bifolia, however, which had become detached long before, remained in Germany, and were ultimately bound up at the end of a large collection of autographs in the hand of Franz Xaver Süssmayr, Mozart's favourite pupil. This collection was sold to the British Museum in February 1884 by List & Francke, a Leipzig firm of booksellers. Now just as for many years Mozart's hand had strongly resembled that of his father, his sole teacher, so, in time, did the hands of several of Mozart's pupils bear a resemblance, however superficial, to his. Thus when the Süssmayr collection was catalogued in the Museum, the last two bifolia of the Mozart rondo were described as part of an imperfect concerto by Süssmayr. Not until the spring of 1980 were they recognised, by Alan Tyson, for what they are. (Nine leaves and two fragments of this scattered Mozart

49

autograph score, out of a probable total of fourteen, are now known to survive.)

As a pendant to this manuscript, it should be mentioned that the collections include three of the numerous cadenzas which Mozart wrote, mostly for his own concertos, but sometimes for those by other composers. One of the latter type is that which Mozart wrote about 1773 for his earlier pasticcio-concerto, K40, of 1767, which was a transcription of three movements of various piano pieces, the first from a sonata by Leontzi Honauer. This cadenza is on one side of the autograph strip of K168a described on p.45. In its margin Mozart noted: 'Zum ersten Stück vom Conzert aus dem D pastigio'. The fragmentary leaf bearing this cadenza is particularly significant because it shows that when Mozart was about seventeen he was still playing the pasticcio dating from his eleventh year. One of the most popular concertos of Mozart's youth seems to have been that in C major, K246, for which he left no fewer than seven cadenzas, three for the first movement and four for the second. A most interesting manuscript comprises two of them, one for each movement. It was acquired from the estate of C. B. Oldman, in commemoration of that distinguished Mozart scholar, who was Principal Keeper of Printed Books in the British Museum from 1948 to 1959.

Another keyboard autograph had an unusual association with two erstwhile members of the Museum staff as private collectors. This is a single leaf of the piano sonata in B flat major, K570, the only one of the entire autograph now known. It comprises the end of the first movement, from bar 65 to bar 209, written on both sides of the leaf and signed on the verso by both Constanze Nissen and her second husband, with the date 1822, and attestation of authenticity in the latter's hand. Once owned by Eric Millar, Keeper of Manuscripts from 1944 to 1947, it was acquired by E. H. W. Meyerstein, already mentioned as a former Assistant Keeper in that Department, who bequeathed it in 1953.

(ii) Vocal

No complete Mozart opera in autograph is in the collections. This is because the scores of all the major ones were in the collection which André's heirs sold to Berlin – all, that is, save one. They kept *Don Giovanni*, and the famous soprano Pauline Viardot-Garcia bought it from them in 1855, for the equivalent of about £180. In his *Musical Sketches* (1869) John Ella states that at some earlier date it had been offered, for a lower price, to the British Museum, which refused that unique opportunity. Viardot-Garcia bequeathed this autograph to the Bibliothèque Nationale in Paris.

The Stefan Zweig collection, however, contains two operatic pieces. One is a two-leaf draft of 'Non so più', in *Le nozze di Figaro*. Mozart headed the

29. Mozart's 'Aria di Cherubino. Scene V'. Opening of a sketch of 'Non so più' in *Le nozze di Figaro*. Autograph. 238 × 320mm.

first leaf: 'Atto i^{mo}. Aria di Cherubino. Scene V' (fig.29). The verso of the second leaf bears a sketch for an aria not found in the score of *Figaro*. The second manuscript is the full autograph score of 'Deh prendi un dolce amplesso', no.3 in the first act of *La clemenza di Tito*, sung by Sesto and Annio. These two leaves seem to have been extracted by Constanze Mozart from the complete score.

One of the gems of the Zweig collection is the autograph of Mozart's best known song *Das Veilchen*, which he wrote on 8 June 1785. It is his only setting of a poem by Goethe, whose name he inscribed at the head. The end of the music is followed by an inscription: 'Eigentum von Wilh. Speyer', he being the musician and banker (1790–1878) who received the autograph as a gift from his friend and teacher J. A. André. The song passed to Speyer's son Edward (already mentioned in connection with the 'Ten quartets'), and when he died, aged nearly 95, in 1934, Zweig added it to his collection.

The numerous canons which Mozart wrote throughout his life were mostly intended either as serious contrapuntal exercises or for use on jocular social occasions. Two of the latter kind are in the Zweig collection: *Difficile lectu mihi Mars* (K559) and *O du eselhafter Peierl* (K560a). Though Mozart entered them both in his catalogue on 2 September 1788 there is reason to think that he wrote them some three years before. Eight serious canons, mostly for soprano voice, are found on one side of the sheet in the Wandering Minstrels' album in the Music Library: probably composed in the summer of 1786, they are untexted, and are identified simply by their number, K508a.

5. Miscellaneous Autographs and Documents

This chapter describes various manuscripts of musical and literary interest, mainly written by Mozart or by others closely associated with him. One is the unique catalogue of his compositions which he kept during the last seven years of his life. Another is the extensive exercise book written by his pupil, Thomas Attwood, to which Mozart made important contributions. There are also copies, written out by Mozart and by his father, of works composed by other musicians. A number of letters round off this miscellany.

'Verzeichnüss aller meiner Werke...'

Earlier in these pages, reference has been made to Mozart's own 'thematic catalogue'. This document passed, with the rest of the autographs in Constanze's possession, to J. A. André, and was ultimately acquired by Stefan Zweig, to become the crown of his Mozart collection. It is a manuscript of rare human interest. The white label on its front cover is inscribed in the composer's hand: 'Verzeichnüss aller meiner Werke, vom Monath Febrario 1784 bis Monath 1 . Wolfgang Amadé Mozart mpia'. ('A list of all my works from the month of February 1784 to the month 1 . Wolfgang Amadé Mozart by my own hand'). The space which he left after the '1' – the thousand-digit in the year – seems most touching. For it suggests that in 1784, Mozart, still only twenty-eight, had every reason to expect that he would live well into the nineteenth century.

He appears to have begun his catalogue as part of an attempt to introduce some order into his hectic, irregular mode of life. (At about the same time he and Constanze started to keep domestic accounts, and he maintained a record of his earnings.) The catalogue is a slim little volume, small quarto in size and bound in the original half-leather and decorated paper sides. As it shows surprisingly few signs of hard wear, it probably stayed on or near Mozart's desk and was not carried about in his pocket. The unruled left-hand page of each opening bears the titles or descriptions of the compositions, and, in the case of the operas, the names of the casts. For some other vocal works he wrote the name of the singer. Each right-hand page was ruled with ten staves grouped in pairs, on which he wrote the first few bars of the music, in short score where necessary. As can be seen in fig.30, each opening thus accommodated five works.

30. Mozart: *Verzeichnüss aller meiner Werke*. The opening shows five entries made in 1788, the middle three being the symphony in G minor, K550 (25 July); the symphony in C major, K551 (10 August); and the song *Beim Auszug in das Feld*, K552 (11 August). Autograph. 210 × 320mm.

The first entry was headed thus: '1784|den 9ten Hornung|Ein Clavier-konzert. Begleitung. . .' (K449). ('1784|9 February| A piano concerto. Accompaniment. . .' (K449).) (There is some reason to believe that Mozart began the catalogue not in February but in about November, and that he wrote the first nine entries retrospectively.) Above each subsequent entry he put only the day and month (see fig.30), and wrote the year only above the first composition entered in each January. In and after 1789, however, he often wrote only the month. For the most part, Mozart maintained his system well; he omitted fewer than a score of works, about half of them being occasional pieces. On the other hand, there are some compositions entered in it which are now completely lost – for instance, an Andante for a violin concerto, K470; an orchestral march, K544; two contredanses, K565; and an aria with orchestra, K569 – the last three falling within the period from June 1788 to January 1789. The final composition recorded is the little Masonic Cantata, K623, which Mozart entered on 15 November 1791, three weeks before he died. No other great master of music kept such a detailed chronological list of such inestimable value.

The Attwood Manuscript

The so-called Attwood Manuscript (K506a) has a unique association with Mozart. Thomas Attwood (1765–1838) (fig.32) was serving as a page in the household of the Prince of Wales (later George IV), when the Prince, himself very musical, noticed the boy's talents and in 1783 sent him to study music in Naples. During the two years he spent there Attwood apparently did not learn a great deal, and so (still, apparently, at the Prince's expense) he went on to Vienna where he became Mozart's pupil in August 1785. During the next sixteen months at least, Mozart gave Attwood many lessons in composition, taking him from the rudiments up to quite advanced forms. The record of Attwood's studies survives in a remarkable manuscript of 148 folios which bear a very large number of corrections, some quite extensive, in Mozart's hand. The manuscript also has touches of human interest. At one point (fig.31) he inserted a message to Attwood about the time of their next lesson, and at another, after crossing out a particularly silly error, Mozart wrote in the margin, twice, 'You are an ass'! (fig.33). The manuscript also contains two complete compositions which Mozart wrote as examples. It passed ultimately to C. B. Oldman, and was bought, some time after his death in 1969, by the British Library. It is worth remembering that Mozart gave these lessons during one of the most busy times of his own creative life, the period when he was writing *Le nozze di Figaro* and some of the greatest concert arias and piano concertos. Oldman aptly summed up the significance of these lessons thus: 'they are valuable not only for the light they throw on the prentice years of

31. *(above)* Part of a page of Attwood's book of musical exercises written under Mozart's supervision. The clefs, the bass lines and figurings are in the hand of Mozart who has also written a message for Attwood, in English, at the end of the third and fourth staves: 'This after noon I am not at home. therefore I pray you to come tomorrow at three and a half. Mozart *mpa*'. 125 × 303mm.

32. *(right)* Thomas Attwood (1765–1838). Unsigned lithograph. 225 × 165mm.

33. Part of a page of Attwood's book of musical exercises, written under Mozart's supervision. Beside a passage which Mozart completed and then mostly cancelled, he wrote twice: 'You are an ass'. 125 × 315mm.

an English composer, but as evidence that Mozart, given an apt and congenial pupil, took his duties as a teacher with the utmost seriousness'.

The Copies

Mozart and his father, like many composers of their day, were inveterate copiers of music. Leopold copied a good deal of his son's and both of them made a lot of copies of works by other composers. They did this partly with the practical aim of providing material for performance, and partly to gain experience by study.

The earliest copy by either father or son now in the collections is one written by Leopold, in his most elegant hand, of the violin part to Wolfgang's sonatas K10–15, published as op.III. This is found with the set of the parts which was presented to Queen Charlotte, the dedicatee, and is now in the Royal Music Library, sumptuously bound in red morocco. The copy was needed because, although there is a separate engraved cello part, that for the violin was printed only in score with the keyboard part.

A manuscript which was long accepted as an original composition of Wolfgang's is the psalm *De profundis clamavi* (K93/Anh.A22). Dating probably from the early 1770s, it is now known to be the work of C. G. Reutter, who was active at St. Stephen's Cathedral in Vienna until his death in 1772.

A most interesting Mozart manuscript was among the fine collection amassed by J. E. Perabo and presented by E. P. Warren in 1928. It contains nineteen substantial named pieces of church music, eighteen by J. E. Eberlin, active as organist and court composer in Salzburg from 1726 up to 1762, and one by Michael Haydn (the younger brother of Joseph) who held various appointments there for some forty years. Both musicians were friends of the Mozarts. All these pieces were accepted as being in

Mozart's hand, but in fact he copied only the *Ave Maria* by Haydn, and all the rest are in Leopold's writing. Even in the early 1770s, the likely period of this manuscript, there was still a considerable resemblance between the two. Michael Haydn appears again in a manuscript deposited on loan by the Royal College of Organists. It was long regarded as a composition by Mozart, but is in fact the beginning (forty-five bars) of a copy of the last movement, in fugal style, of a symphony by Haydn in D major. Mozart's copy can perhaps be dated, on the basis of its paper-type, to about 1783, though other evidence suggests a rather earlier date of 1778–79. This manuscript was bought in Vienna by John Ella in January 1846 and was bequeathed by him to the Royal College.

The Letters

The Stefan Zweig collection has five letters in Mozart's hand. That which he wrote to Professor Anton Klein on 21 May 1785 is of great importance as a serious statement of one of Mozart's most cherished artistic beliefs. Klein, an ex-Jesuit, was a university lecturer on philosophy and aesthetics. He also wrote plays, one of which, *Kaiser Rudolf von Habsburg*, he sent to Mozart, suggesting that he set it to music. In this letter Mozart, while declining the offer with regret, deplores the decline of German opera in Vienna, and states the urgent need for its revival at a higher standard.

The other four letters were all written to his cousin in Augsburg, Maria Anna Thekla Mozart (1758–1841) – generally known as 'the Bäsle' – at intervals from November 1777 to May 1779. All are largely in a playful, amorous vein, full of puns and word-play, and show how Mozart made her the butt of the type of scatological humour that seems to have been quite general in southern Germany at that time. (Traces of it are also found in letters written by both Mozart's parents). The letter that Mozart wrote to his cousin on 28 February 1778 also contains a notable example of his capacity for whimsical, dream-like fantasy, expressed in a weird tale about a shepherd and his 11,000 sheep.

The British Library's collections have an important letter from Mozart to his sister, dated 19 December 1787, recording the great success of *Don Giovanni,* and telling her of his recent appointment as Chamber Composer to the Emperor Joseph II. There is also a charming example of the purely domestic type of letter which make the Mozart family's correspondence so fascinating – one which Leopold Mozart wrote to his daughter from Munich on 15 February 1786, two years after her marriage. Among much musical gossip, he tells her how much he enjoyed hearing a young musician give a brilliant performance of Wolfgang's piano sonata and fantasy in C minor, K457 and K475.

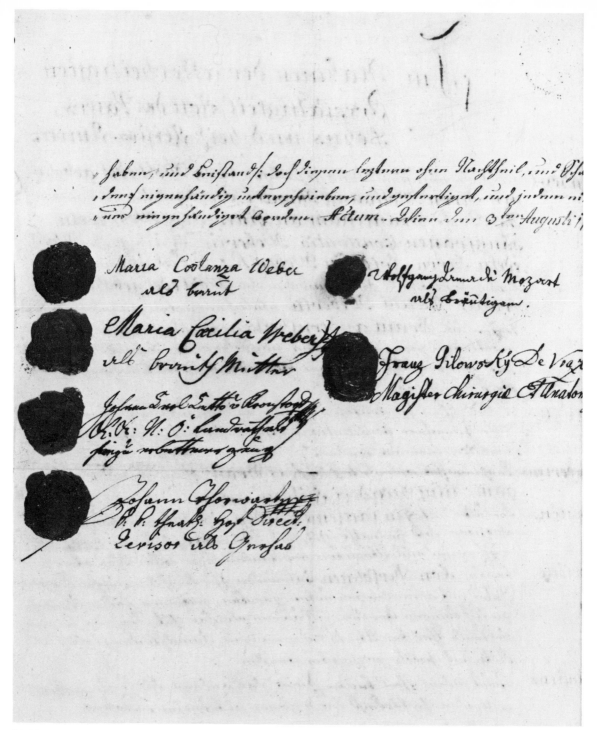

34. Mozart's marriage contract, 3 August 1782. The upper part of the verso signed by Maria Costanza [sic] Weber as bride; Wolfgang Amadé Mozart as bridegroom; Maria Cecilia Weber as bride's mother; two witnesses; and Johann Thorwart, as the bride's guardian. Of the six seals, Mozart's alone lacks a coat of arms. 210 × 215mm.

Mozart's Marriage Contract

This important document is in the Zweig collection. It was signed by the composer, Constanze, her mother Maria Cecilia Weber, and several witnesses, on 3 August 1782 (fig.34). The second and third clauses in the contract record that the bride brought a dowry of 500 gulden, and that the groom augmented it by 1000 gulden, the total of 1500 gulden to pass to the survivor of the marriage. That sum, at least, Constanze received when she was widowed nine years later.

A possible Autograph by 'Nannerl' Mozart

Musical autographs in the hand of Mozart's sister are rarely found outside libraries in Austria and Germany, and because few are signed, most can only be identified as hers on the evidence of the handwriting. This is the case with one of the manuscripts deposited on loan by the Royal College of Organists. It takes the form of an undated arpeggio exercise written on a sheet some 120 × 304 mm, and was given to John Ella in Vienna in December 1845 by the musicologist Aloys Fuchs, who assured him that Wolfgang had written it in 1762! Ella had the sheet framed and glazed, and on the strength of this erroneous assurance, inscribed Fuchs' statement at the foot of it, and round the generous margin of the mount also wrote a sort of calendar of Wolfgang's early life. It is, however, neither in Wolfgang's hand, nor in his father's. But as the writing does correspond in several respects – though not in all – to other authenticated autographs by Nannerl, the sheet may be tentatively accepted as an untypical example of her hand. Though of uncertain date, it seems likely to exemplify the kind of exercise she wrote under her father's supervision.

6. From Manuscript to Print

Virtually all Mozart's music is now easily available in print. Besides the *Neue Mozart Ausgabe* (the definitive scholarly edition begun in 1955 and due for completion within the next decade or so), there is a vast quantity of other publications – various collections and selections large and small, an immense range of single works, extracts and arrangements, obtainable from music publishers and their agents all over the world. While this state of affairs is taken for granted today, it is worth remembering that it was all the result of a slow, complex process which began quite soon after Mozart's death, but did not reach the end of the first phase until over a century later.

During Mozart's life, there were published only some seventy original editions of his works, a very small part of the whole. Though these editions included five piano concertos, a few symphonies, and one complete opera – *Die Entführung aus dem Serail* – in vocal score (fig.35), the rest was all in smaller forms, largely chamber works and piano music, plus a few songs. Soon after Mozart's death his mature operas grew steadily in popularity all over Europe, prompting their widespread publication in vocal score; a few full scores were also printed. But the bulk of his music remained unavailable to its wider potential public until the later 1790s. As we have seen, Constanze Mozart owned and retained the musical autographs, and in 1798 Breitkopf & Härtel persuaded her to sell them a small number which they used, supplemented by manuscript copies and what they could find in print, to issue their *Oeuvres complettes*. The scheme of this undertaking was ambitious, but curiously assorted, and was planned in three sections. The first, which comprised works for piano solo, chamber music with a piano part and some songs and canons, ran to seventeen finely printed 'cahiers', each with a handsomely engraved vignette titlepage (figs.36 and 37). The second section attempted scores of large-scale vocal works, and amounted to the Requiem, two other masses, and *Don Giovanni*. In the last group there were twenty piano concertos, in parts, and a dozen string quartets: some operatic arias in vocal score with instrumental parts seem to have been issued as a supplement. When this enterprise came to an end in 1806, there was still a large residue of Mozart unpublished, and although other firms in Germany, France and England imitated the Breitkopf edition, they, too, virtually eschewed all his compositions in larger forms.

As already mentioned in Chapter 3, it was only after 1799, when Constanze Mozart sold the bulk of her husband's autographs to Johann Anton André, that the scope of publication could be enlarged. Though

35. Titlepage of the vocal score of *Die Entführung aus dem Serail*. First edition. 1782. 230 × 290mm.

André gradually issued quite a number of important works, largely instrumental ones, in parts, he worked virtually single-handed. So it was a slow process and ultimately his zeal as a publisher gave way to an increasing interest in the study of the collection of autographs as a Mozart archive. After the mid-1820s André published only a few more Mozart editions, though some are of considerable critical importance.

Meanwhile, as a little more of his music became available, people wanted to know more about his life. The earliest biography, which took the form of an obituary notice, was written by A. H. F. von Schlichtegroll, and appeared in the *Nekrolog auf das Jahr 1791*. It was reprinted in 1794 as a separate pamphlet called *Mozarts Leben*. In 1798 F. X. Niemetschek completed his *Leben des K. K. Kapellmeisters Wolfgang Gottlieb Mozart*, which was published in Prague, and went into a second edition in 1808. These rare books and a few similar ones issued in the next two decades – copies are to be found in the British Library – were bare biographical outlines:

they said very little about the music except the operas, and mentioned the rest in general, mostly quantitative terms.

There were two main reasons for this unpropitious start. The art of musical biography was then still very much in its infancy, and in Mozart's case all the important sources and documents were still owned, as had been the autographs, by Constanze. She carefully preserved what her first husband had inherited from his father and had added to himself – letters, travel diaries, family recollections and a mass of other papers. Naturally she was reluctant to release them for general use. Ultimately she entrusted the task of using these sources for a major biography to her second husband, Georg Nikolaus Nissen, who began work in 1823 and left the book almost finished when he died in 1826. Breitkopf & Härtel published it in 1828 (fig.38). Being in effect an 'official' biography, the book enjoyed a wide *succès d'estime,* and its subscription list, which ran to some 650 names, included eight crowned heads of Germany and many princes and dukes. Besides booksellers and music publishers, the list named numerous

36. Mozart.
Oeuvres complettes.
[1801].
Cah. IX.
Titlepage vignette engraved by Amadeus Wenzel Böhm after Vincenz Georg Kininger.
254 × 340mm.

musicians, among them Mendelssohn. As many subscribers took more than one copy, the total printing exceeded 1000.

What Nissen produced was, by any standards, a very large book: its main section ran to 702 pages, followed by an appendix of 219 more. By quoting many unpublished letters and other documents, he built up a fairly detailed account of much of Mozart's life, and to supplement the chronology he printed the *Verzeichnüss* of music composed from 1784 onwards. But for the earlier years, especially after 1768 (the year when Leopold made a list of all his son's juvenile compositions) Nissen's work was unavoidably imprecise and incomplete. Meanwhile, as just mentioned, André had been making a detailed study of Mozart autographs and realised the need for a systematic list of the works composed between 1768 and 1784. This presented great difficulties, not least because many of them bore no date. From the early 1820s he made several attempts to construct a thematic catalogue, but the only one to reach some degree of completeness was that which he finished in 1833. (A copy of it is in the British Library.)

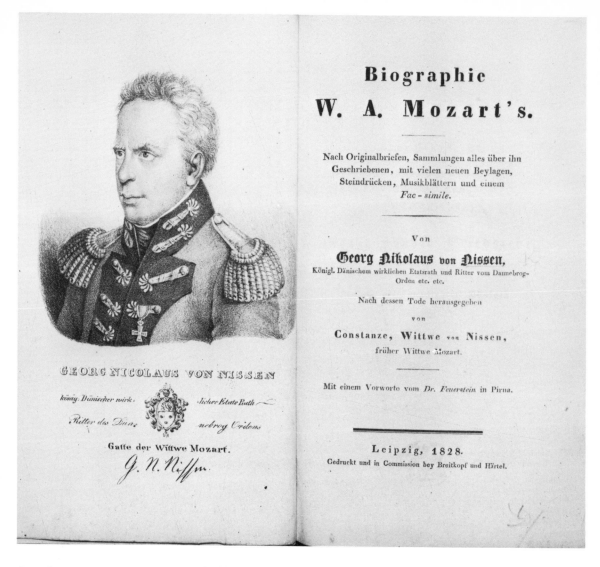

Biographie
W. A. Mozart's.

Nach Originalbriefen, Sammlungen alles über ihn
Geschriebenen, mit vielen neuen Beylagen,
Steindrücken, Musikblättern und einem
Fac - simile.

Von

Georg Nikolaus von Nissen,
Königl. Dänischem wirklichen Etatsrath und Ritter vom Dannebrog-
Orden etc. etc.

Nach dessen Tode herausgegeben

von

Constanze, Wittwe von Nissen,
früher Wittwe Mozart.

Mit einem Vorworte vom Dr. Feuerstein in Pirna.

Leipzig, 1828.
Gedruckt und in Commission bey Breitkopf und Härtel.

GEORG NICOLAUS VON NISSEN

könig. Dänischer wirk.   licher Etats Rath
Ritter des Dan-   nebrog Ordens

Gatte der Wittwe Mozart.

G. N. Nissen.

Another attempt to put Mozart's work in order was made by Aloys Fuchs, who drew up a chronological list of it in 1837. During all this time, publication of the music still proceeded very slowly, and little progress was made in biography.

Nineteen years after Nissen's book was published, another writer, of far greater distinction, took up the biographical challenge again. This was Otto Jahn, a renowned German classical scholar of unusual versatility, who began work in 1847 and spent several years travelling widely to study Mozart collections, public and private. The first of the four volumes of his great critical biography appeared in 1856, the centenary of Mozart's birth, and the last in 1859. The one technical weakness of his book was that it necessarily lacked any coherent system of numbering by which Mozart's

38. First edition of the life of Mozart by Georg Nikolaus Nissen (1761–1826), 1828, edited by his widow Constanze. Nissen's portrait, not Mozart's, appeared as the frontispiece. 200 × 240mm.

compositions, published or unpublished, could be referred to and identified. Yet even while Jahn was at work, such a system was being drawn up by one of the most remarkable men who has ever laboured in the service of Mozart scholarship – Ludwig Ritter von Köchel (fig.39).

Köchel was trained in law, but early developed a scientific interest that led him to specialise in botany and mineralogy, two fields of learning in which he won wide fame. He was also a man of some means, with a love of music in general and of Mozart in particular. When in 1851 his attention was drawn to the lack of any unified, systematic knowledge about the corpus of Mozart's music, he began to apply his scientific mind to the many problems involved. André's heirs lent Köchel the former's thematic catalogue of 1833 and presumably gave him access to the autographs still in their possession. But many of these were undated, and those of other

39. Ludwig Ritter von Köchel (1800–1877). Photograph, with his signature.
115 × 100mm.

67

known works lost (especially juvenilia) or dispersed. Köchel had therefore to try to find any extant manuscript copies or, failing these, to trace and identify first editions. The largest and most daunting part of his task was to create a valid chronological sequence for all the works (448, in his ultimate reckoning) which Mozart composed before February 1784. Ten years' unremitting effort produced the epochal catalogue, *Chronologisch-thematisches Verzeichnis sämtlicher Tonwerke Wolfgang Amade Mozarts*, which Breitkopf published in 1862.

The scheme that Köchel devised for each composition is a marvel of simplicity, clarity and originality. After the number given to each he put the date of composition, known or conjectural, the title, and the opening

40. Entry for Mozart's string quartet in D major, K499, in the first edition of Köchel's catalogue, 1862. 265 × 156mm.

bars of the music. Then came the location of the autograph or other manuscript source, followed by the first edition, and lastly miscellaneous information, under 'Anmerkung'. This included reference to any relevant passage in Nissen, or in Jahn, the dedicatee of Köchel's catalogue, who incorporated its numbering in the second, 1869, edition of his biography. A specimen of Köchel's scheme can be seen in fig.40, which shows the entry for the 'Hoffmeister' quartet, K499. To the main section of the catalogue, Köchel prefixed a thematic synopsis of Mozart's music, arranged in twenty-three categories, each work being identified by a number corresponding to the one in the catalogue proper.

Köchel's catalogue was the first of its kind and served as the basic model for many others. He had no reason to expect that posterity would use the first letter of his surname, with his numbering (now supplemented, especially for early works, by a second, corrective number) to identify each and every Mozart composition. He was the first man in any field of literature to win immortality in this way. His catalogue appeared at a most propitious moment. Definitive publication of the complete works of the great masters of music had begun – J. S. Bach in 1850, Handel in 1859 and Beethoven in 1862. Now that scholarly bibliography and biography of Mozart had at last gone hand in hand, it was only natural that publication of the music should follow. But interest was still very limited, and even Breitkopf & Härtel could not undertake a complete edition unaided. It was then that Köchel rendered the last of his great services to Mozart. Having devoted much time to seeking patrons among the German monarchy (the list – rather like Nissen's – ultimately included eight crowned heads of Europe), among musicians and the aristocracy, he himself gave the equivalent in Austrian money of some £1,500 – a large sum in those days – as a subsidy in 1875.

The Breitkopf edition was entitled: *Wolfgang Amadeus Mozarts Werke*. When publication began in 1877, the scheme used was based, with some modification of sequence, on the twenty-three categories which Köchel had devised himself. By 1883 this great edition was largely finished, yet the number of subscribers was only ninety-three. A supplement of rediscovered, unfinished and doubtful works followed at intervals up to 1905. When Köchel died, on 3 June 1877, Mozart's Requiem, which Brahms had prepared for the Breitkopf edition, was performed at his funeral.

In 1964 there appeared the most recent of the three substantial revisions of Köchel's catalogue. While his basic plan was retained, each revision added much new or corrective information – a changed location of the autograph, the discovery of significant manuscript copies, more details of the title and date of the first and later editions, references to an ever growing range of Mozart literature, and the like. Fig.41 illustrates the extent of all this information, again for the 'Hoffmeister' quartet, and a comparison with fig.40 shows how the range of bibliographical knowledge about Mozart's works and its presentation have expanded in just over a century.

Just as Köchel has evolved in course of time, so too have the standards of the complete edition, now known as *Alte Mozart Ausgabe – A.M.A.* – to distinguish it from the *Neue Mozart Ausgabe – N.M.A.* – mentioned at the beginning of this chapter. The *N.M.A.* has reached a level of scholarly excellence unimaginable a century ago, for a variety of reasons. International co-operation has led to the discovery of some long-lost autographs and of important early manuscript copies. Known autographs have been re-examined. Intensive study has produced a new understanding of the changes in Mozart's handwriting, and the features which distinguish it

41. Entry for Mozart's string quartet in D major, K499, in the sixth edition of Köchel's catalogue, 1964.
270 × 170mm.

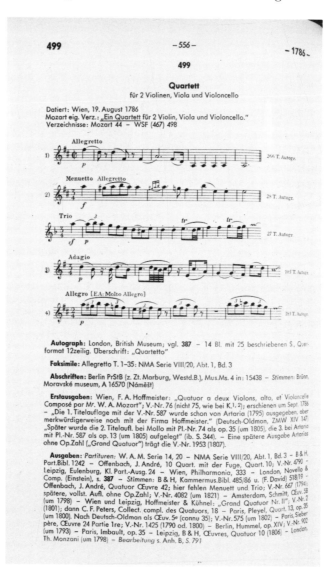

from his father's. This work, combined with the study of the various types of music paper which Mozart used (its stave-ruling, the watermarks, and the ink), has contributed, as already mentioned, to a refinement of chronology and a new, complex range of knowledge. The general result is a notable increase in editorial precision.

One example must suffice here – the revised text of the opening melody of the finale of the string quintet in D major, K593. Mozart composed it as a smooth, descending chromatic scale, which gave the movement much of its distinctive character. Before Artaria issued the first edition in May 1793, this theme was cancelled, at all its thirty recurrences, throughout the autograph, and altered to a zig-zag type of melody which, though making the music easier to play, gave it a diatonic flavour. The editors of *A.M.A.*, believing mistakenly that Mozart himself had made the alteration, printed the music in this version, to agree with the first edition. Fig.42 shows the opening of the development as it is in *A.M.A.* But careful scrutiny of the autograph recently showed that the hand which made this alteration was not Mozart's but another's – perhaps someone in the publishing house. Thus *N.M.A.* restored Mozart's chromatic original melody, as in fig.43 (the corresponding passage to fig.42), much to the benefit of the music.

Such, in outline, is the intricate process by which, during the last two hundred years or so, Mozart's music has become available in print. It remains to say something of its representation and extent in the British Library's collection. In terms of quantity – the Mozart heading in the catalogue contains over 8000 entries – it is one of the largest in any national library, and is especially rich in editions published before 1840. That it is also one of the most important is due to two principal reasons. First, those responsible for the collections of printed music from the 1840s onwards had continually done their best to build up the holding of the Viennese classics in general and Mozart in particular. Secondly, what had become a very good collection was greatly enhanced in 1946 when the Trustees of the British Museum purchased, for £120,000, the Paul Hirsch Music Library.

Paul Hirsch (1881–1951) (fig.44) was a German industrialist who left Frankfurt on the Main in 1936 to come to England where he settled in Cambridge with his library. When he began collecting music, about 1897, some of his first purchases were of Mozart, his favourite composer. This collection grew so rapidly that in 1906, to mark the 150th anniversary of the composer's birth, he issued a special catalogue, the first ever devoted to a private Mozart collection. In the next forty years, its growth kept pace with that of his very extensive library (which ultimately amounted to some 20,000 items of music and musical literature). It included some 850 items of Mozart's music, and nearly 500 volumes of criticism and biography, among which were many rare early books and pamphlets (see p.63).

The British Library's collection as a whole reflects many different

42. Finale of Mozart's string quintet in D major, K593 in the *Alte Mozart Ausgabe*, 1883, showing the 'zig-zag' version of the first subject, erroneously derived from an early emendation of Mozart's autograph. 145 × 210mm.

43. Finale of Mozart's string quintet in D major, K593, in the *Neue Mozart Ausgabe*, 1967, showing the development of the chromatic first subject as in the autograph. 140 × 210mm.

aspects of Mozart's music, of which only a few can be mentioned here. In practical terms it shows the endlessly fascinating variety of the work done by editors and publishers to make the music available for music-lovers to play and sing, in an extraordinary variety of forms. There is, for instance, an edition of most of *Don Giovanni* issued by Schott of Mainz in about 1806, arranged for flute, violin, viola and cello, which must have satisfied a demand from chamber or domestic players of a kind now hard to imagine. Rather more usual are the numerous popular editions of Mozart's concertos and symphonies in arrangements for piano duet. In the time before sound recording, broadcasting, and relatively easy travel to concerts, such publications provided the only way in which amateurs could explore and enjoy these works. Again, the collections are rich in the pocket

44. Photograph of Paul Hirsch in his study at 10, Adams Road, Cambridge, *c*.1950, by Count Leo Lanckarónski. 125 × 70mm.

scores which were issued from the early nineteenth century onwards. They vary in size from the string quintets printed in octavo by Pleyel of Paris in about 1810, to the symphonies in a slightly larger format by Breitkopf in the 1820s, and the chamber music published in delightful duodecimo size which appeared under the imprint of Heckel of Mannheim from the 1850s onwards. The collections also contain a large number of pocket scores of Mozart printed all over Europe throughout the twentieth century, which testify to the incessant demand for his music in a format suitable for personal study.

Historically, the collections are no less comprehensive and interesting, thanks largely to the fact that the Hirsch Library is so rich in first and early editions. We have already seen in the case of the 'Haydn' quartets (p.40) what the significance of the first edition is in relation to the autograph. Such publications assume an even greater importance when the autograph is lost and the first edition is the sole source for the music. This applies not only to Mozart's juvenilia such as the sonatas op.I, II and III (K6,7; K8,9, and K10–15) but also a fair number of mature works. Such for example are the sinfonia concertante for violin and viola, the piano quartet in E flat major, K493, and the string trio in E flat major: all these autographs are lost, but the first editions, in parts, can be found (mostly, though not solely) in the Hirsch Library. So, too, is the song *Lied beim Auszug in das Feld*, K552, which Mozart composed just after the 'Jupiter' symphony, in August 1788. Until 1906 only the incipit was known, as given in his thematic catalogue (see fig.30). But in that year Hirsch acquired a copy of the song in the form of a small printed sheet which had been noticed by a dealer bound up in a miscellaneous volume. As was later discovered, this song had been issued, in the month of its composition, as a supplement to the journal *Angenehme und lehrreiche Beschäftigung für Kinder in ihren Freistunden*. Three other Mozart songs associated with children are in the collection 'Frühlingslieder', part of *Lieder-sammlung für Kinder und Kinderfreunde am Clavier* (Vienna, 1791), which has a charming titlepage (fig.45). This is the only source for the songs K596, 597 and 598. Again, the first edition of the fantasia for piano in D minor (K397), published in 1804, with the title 'Fantaisie d'introduction morceau detaché' is of primary interest, the more so because Hirsch's study of his copy led him to a significant textual discovery. He noticed that here the music ended on a pause, and lacked the last ten bars printed in all subsequent editions. When Hirsch found that this addition first appeared in cahier XVII of the *Oeuvres complettes* published in 1806 by Breitkopf & Härtel, he concluded that these bars had been added at their instance, probably by A. E. Müller, the composer who worked as their adviser and head reader. Hirsch showed that Breitkopf & Härtel did this because otherwise the end of an attractive and very saleable piece of music would have been left hanging, so to speak, on the chord of a dominant seventh.

LIEDERSAMMLUNG

FÜR

KINDER UND KINDERFREUNDE

AM CLAVIER.

FRÜHLINGSLIEDER.

WIEN,

GEDRUCKT BEY IGNAZ ALBERTI, K. K. PRIV. BUCHDRUCKER. MDCCXCI.

45. Collection of children's songs, including the first edition of Mozart's 'Three German songs' K596, 597, 598. 1791. The titlepage vignette engraved by Klemens Kohl after Johann Christian Sambach. 195 × 265mm.

A few first editions, besides being the unique source, have various personal associations with Mozart. One such is the masonic cantata *Die Maurerfreude*, K471, whose titlepage (fig.46) makes a notable statement of his membership of the craft to which he was so long devoted. This titlepage needs some clarification. Mozart composed the cantata to honour an important scientific discovery made by his friend and patron Baron Ignaz von Born, who was a freemason and in 1785 Master of the lodge 'Zur wahren Eintracht' (the 'True Concord'). His name and Mozart's appear on the titlepage with dots, in the usual masonic style, to indicate the omitted letters. The name of Mozart's lodge, 'Gekrönte Hoffnung im Orient' (the 'Crowned Hope'), where the cantata was first performed, is given on this titlepage with a similar omission and partially abridged.

Another type of first edition may owe its interest to a close association between Mozart and the musician responsible for it, as in the case of *Storace's Collection of original Harpsichord Music*, issued in London from 1787 to 1789 by Birchall & Andrews for Stephen Storace, who, with his sister Nancy and their friend Thomas Attwood, had known Mozart well earlier in that decade. This anthology included the first English edition of

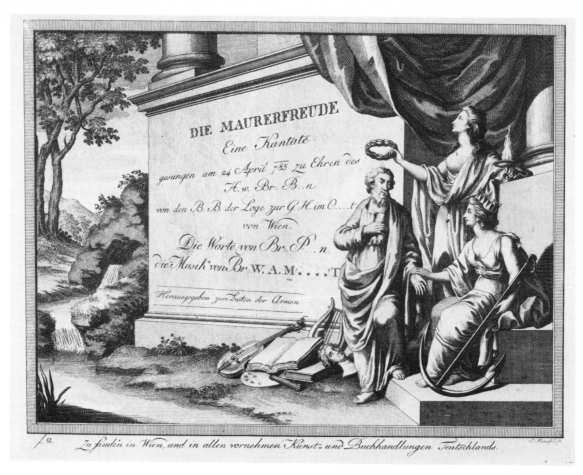

46. Titlepage of
Mozart's masonic
cantata *Die
Maurerfreude*,
K471.
First edition. 1785.
Engraved by
Sebastian Mansfeld
after Ignaz
Unterberger.
243 × 356mm.

the latter's piano quartet in E flat major, which appeared in 1787, only a
few months after the Viennese first edition, but from a different source,
perhaps an early manuscript copy procured with Mozart's help. More
importantly, in July 1789, Storace published the first edition anywhere of
the piano trio in G major, K564, for which the composer himself must have
sent a manuscript to London. The British Library's copy of this anthology
is particularly interesting as having been deposited in the British Museum
by copyright at the time of publication, and is the earliest music of Mozart
acquired in this way.

Whatever the degree of interest we now find in Mozart's music as
published in his lifetime and for some decades after, we should not forget
that most editions were primarily issued for a sound commercial purpose –
at least to cover the cost of production, and at best to make a profit. To this
end, many of them were supplied with very attractive titlepages designed
to catch the customer's eye. Some were engraved in a simple calligraphic
style, perhaps with the text framed in an elegant decorated border (see
fig.19). Others were pictorially embellished in a neo-classical or romantic

SIX SONATES

Pour le Clavecin, ou Pianoforte avec l'accompagnement d'un Violon

Dediés A Mademoiselle

IOSEPHE D'AURNHAMER

par

WOLFG. AMADEE MOZART

Oeuvre II.

Publié, et se vendent chez Artaria Compl a Vienne.

22

47. Titlepage of
Mozart's violin
sonatas, K296,
376–380.
First edition. 1781.
235 × 320mm.

manner with a symbolic scene or objects. This can be well seen in the titlepage to *Die Maurerfreude* (fig.46), in which the design includes the masonic symbol of a broken statue. Another distinguished Viennese titlepage was produced for the six violin sonatas published in 1781 (fig.47). Besides whole-page illustrated titlepages, vignettes were much favoured, as exemplified in the two cahiers of the Breitkopf 'complete' edition shown in figs.36 and 37.

Other publishers preferred a style which could offer an illustration of some aspect of the music or illumine its quality by some kind of visual allusion. When in *c.*1801 J. A. André issued the first edition of Mozart's *Musikalischer Spass*, that splendid satire on clumsy, lumpish composition, he commissioned an artist to caricature the six players in military uniform, poring over the parts laid on a table (fig.48). The allusive type of titlepage is well exemplified in a scarce English edition of the 'Jupiter' symphony, in a vignette which shows the god in the act of hurling a thunderbolt (fig.49). It was appropriate that this illustration, and the title, appeared for the first time in an English edition, for the sobriquet 'Jupiter' was probably devised

77

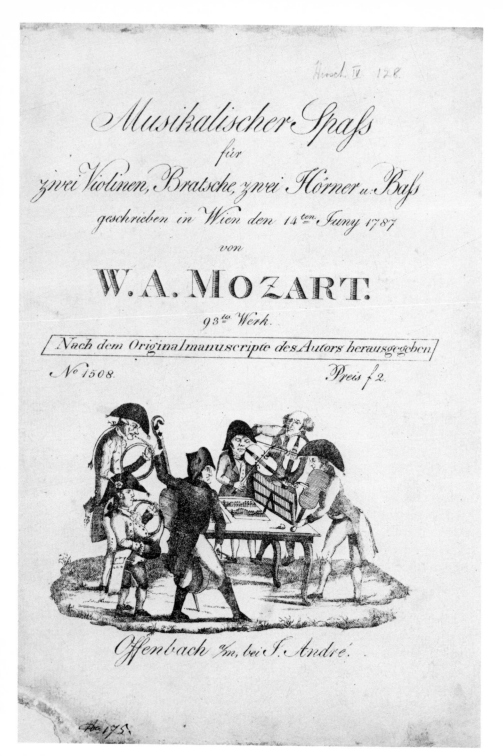

48. Titlepage of Mozart's *Musikalischer Spass*, K522. First edition. *c*.1801. With a satirical lithographed vignette, signed: F.H. 335 × 240mm.

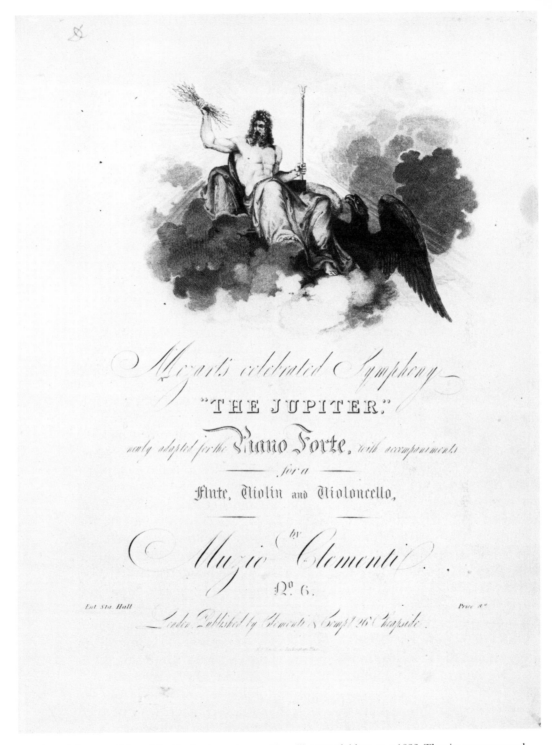

49. The only known edition of the 'Jupiter' symphony with an illustrated titlepage. *c.*1823. The vignette engraved by W. Collard. 235 × 335mm.

by Johann Peter Salomon who, long before his death in 1815, was resident in London and became friendly with Clementi, the arranger of this edition and its publisher.

Because the collections of printed music have been built up over a long period and are fairly representative of the main stream of music publishing, they offer some striking evidence of Mozart's enduring popularity (as of course they would for other great composers). This could be judged from a considerable range of different works: two contrasting ones may suffice here – unusual arrangements, and operas.

The practice of publishing Mozart's music in adaptations, many of which seem bizarre by any standard, began quite early in the nineteenth century. They can be found in the British Library's collections in some quantity, and can be considered here in several distinctive groups. It was in 1812 that William Gardiner published his *Sacred Melodies from Haydn, Mozart and Beethoven:* one of the Mozart pieces was 'Batti, batti', from *Don Giovanni,* reset to the text 'Gently Lord, O gently lead us'. Not long after, the famous recitative and rondo, 'Ch'io mi scordi di te' and 'Non temer', K505 – the rondo much abridged – appeared with French words 'D'une fausse pitié', and 'Eh pourquoi me faire un crime' in a Parisian pasticcio opera, *La prise de Jéricho.* In 1940 'Secondate, aurette amiche', from *Così fan tutte,* was published in New York for women's chorus with a text beginning 'On Wings of Faith'.

As an early example of an instrumental piece derived from a largely vocal one, there are the *Moscow & Livonian Waltzes,* arranged for piano from *Die Zauberflöte* and issued in London about 1820. A favourite melodic source for arrangements is the last two movements of Mozart's piano sonata in A, K331. Of the 'alla turca' finale, the collections have no fewer than forty-seven editions, many for strange mediums. Quite recently, it has been issued as a singing exercise. The andante of this sonata was issued in about 1827 as a song, *Hymn to the Virgin,* the words being by the publisher, Thomas Holloway. It appeared as an anthem, *Lord our God,* in 1911, and as a duet, *A Fisher's Night Song,* in 1902. Another favourite andante source is the lyrical slow movement of the piano trio in E major, K542. As a song, it appeared in 1822 arranged by C. E. Horn, entitled *Sweet Music, wake the Day,* and again in 1874 as *When the favored Dove of Noah.* Stranger still, perhaps, is the transmutation, in 1835, of the solemn March of the Priests from *Die Zauberflöte* into a song with a text of six lines from Juvenal's tenth satire, beginning with the famous words 'Orandum est ut sit mens sana in corpore sano'. It was not, however, always melodies in a slow tempo which interested arranger and publisher. A theme from the presto of the 'Prague' symphony attracted one Fanny Steers who adapted it as a song to the words *The Last Links are broken;* the earliest of the six editions in the collections appeared in 1830, and the last in 1866.

An arrangement from one instrumental form to another is quite common and often curious. Such is the piano solo version of the romanza of the D minor piano concerto, produced by Wilhelm Czerny with the title *St. Valentine's Dream: a tender love ditty,* in 1880. Of more recent, almost topical interest, is the simplified version of the slow movement of another piano concerto, the C major, K467, for the 'Elvira Madigan' theme in the film of that name (1974).

What view Mozart himself would have taken of such use of his music is a matter for speculation. But it is interesting to find that his younger son, Wolfgang Amadeus, felt no scruples at all. In 1842, when asked to provide music for the ceremonial unveiling of a memorial to his father in Salzburg, what he produced, and later published, was simply entitled *Festchor zur Enthüllung de Mozart-Denkmals in Salzburg.* This was an acknowledged pot-pourri of his father's music, with a banal text by himself. Moreover, on the titlepage the younger Mozart made an emphatic claim to copyright in the work, something almost unknown to his father!

All these pieces and innumerable orthodox arrangements were relatively short and therefore cheap to produce, unlike such works as entire operas. Nevertheless, the regular re-publication of Mozart's later masterpieces in this class shows that the cost must have been generally justified. The one which beyond all others – even *Die Zauberflöte* – is most numerous in the British Library's collections is *Don Giovanni.* There are ten editions in full score, seventy-two in vocal score, and another twenty arranged more or less complete for piano solo.

As to the number of copies printed in any one edition of a complete opera, there seems now, at least for the earlier nineteenth century, to be little evidence. But we may guess that some were quite large. The Hirsch Library has a vocal score of *Così fan tutte,* published by Meyer of Brunswick about 1830, which includes a list of 1329 subscribers scattered all over Europe. If we may add the few hundred copies printed for general sale, this was quite a large printing for an opera then far less popular than *Don Giovanni.* The average edition of the latter would perhaps have run to some 2000 copies. This and other evidence suggests that Mozart's operas probably enjoyed a popularity far exceeding that of his symphonies, concertos or chamber music. One particular reason for this is that while both the vocal and the instrumental music were memorable for their melodies, the vocal scores of the operas had in addition a special appeal of their own.

7. Some Images of the Operas

The proliferation of Mozart's operas in vocal score that took place from the last decade of the eighteenth century onwards was of course directly related to the phenomenal rash of productions that broke out in theatres all over Europe. Very few of these scores are of any textual significance, since each was simply copied either from an earlier edition or from a random manuscript. While most of them also lack typographical distinction, there is a small number which stand out in that they are embellished with a scene from the opera.

This feature takes various forms. It may be a vignette on a titlepage, or a whole-page frontispiece preceding it. The publication may consist of a single opera, or of a group of them, generally six. In addition to a musical score, similar illustrations occur in pocket books and even as entirely self-contained editions of theatrical designs. All these types are found in the British Library's collections, and are illustrated here by examples selected within a limiting date of about 1830, that is the four decades following Mozart's death.

The purpose of embellishing the edition was to enhance its interest by offering to the purchaser an attractive picture which, even more vividly than the music itself, might remind him of something that could recreate in his mind's eye an image of what he had seen on the stage. Music shops were sometimes not far from the opera house. Since the enterprising publisher aimed at a high standard, he might secure the services of a well-known artist and a distinguished engraver. What adds to the interest of some of these operatic illustrations is that they appear to be the only known example of the artist's work in this specialised field.

In terms of realism, it does not generally seem possible to relate a particular illustration with absolute certainty to a contemporary performance. But the artist may have had access to stage designers' sketches as the basis for his work. He could thus reproduce costumes, action and a little scenery with sufficient accuracy to attract the purchaser. The illustrations may then be of some documentary interest for the local style of production, and the more valuable because so few original designs from these forty years have survived. For this reason, apart from any aesthetic interest, we should be grateful to the publishers who unintentionally contributed something to the visual side of operatic history.

It is regrettable that no illustrated edition of a Mozart opera appeared in his lifetime: the only complete one of any kind so issued, *Die Entführung aus dem Serail*, has, as already mentioned, a purely decorative titlepage (see fig.35). But there is one important and highly relevant publication which Mozart must have seen – the first libretto of *Die Zauberflöte*. It is the only one for any of his operas printed in his lifetime which contains illustrations. There are two of them. One shows a costume design for the feathered figure of Papageno (fig.50), with the bird-cage on his back and a temple in the distance. The other appears to be a composite representation of a cavern crowded with symbols of freemasonry – a star, an urn with intertwined serpents on its surface, a broken statue, a shovel, a masonic square and so on (fig.51). Both these pictures were engraved by Ignaz Alberti, the publisher of the libretto, who, like Mozart, was a freemason and indeed a member of the same lodge, the 'Crowned Hope'. Comparison with some extant scenes from a Viennese production of 1793 (by which time the sets and costumes had probably changed little) suggests that Alberti's engravings reproduce some features of the original production. The cavern scene, which may well allude to the set for Act II Scene 28, probably displayed a more selective use of masonic symbolism. But the pictures in this libretto, which was doubtless on sale at the Theater an der Wien, would have reminded opera-goers of what they had seen on the stage.

Although the first illustrated vocal scores of Mozart's operas only began to appear in the mid-1790s, from then onwards their number increased steadily. The British Library has a good many of them, especially in the Hirsch collection. Since only a selection can be reproduced in these pages, it has been limited to one scene from each of the seven operas of Mozart's maturity. For the ever popular *Don Giovanni*, the favourite scene is that in the finale at the moment when the statue grips the unrepentant Don by the hand. Less well-known but equally attractive is an unsigned vignette of *c*.1810 showing the cemetery scene early in Act II ('O statua gentilissima') where the Don compels Leporello to address the statue of the Commendatore (fig.52). The picture shown – the original is an unusual pale green – conveys something of the eeriness of this chilling encounter.

La clemenza di Tito, far more popular in the decades following Mozart's death than at any time during the later nineteenth century, was the subject of quite a number of illustrations. One of the most vivid is the frontispiece to a vocal score of about 1795: it shows the burning of the Roman Capitol, at the end of Act I (fig.53). The costumes are strictly classical. *Idomeneo*, on the other hand, though also based on a classical story, was far less often staged and therefore published infrequently. Here the collections offer a more limited choice. The charming vignette (fig.54) is from an edition of about 1796–7, and seems to represent the trio sung by Idomeneo, Idamante and Electra near the end of Act II, as the latter two embark from Crete for Greece.

All the foregoing are from operas published singly: some other fine

50. Costume design for Papageno, from the first edition of the libretto of *Die Zauberflöte*, 1791. Engraving by Ignaz Alberti. 158 × 95mm.

51. Imaginary scene in *Die Zauberflöte* from the first edition of the libretto, 1791, showing an entrance to a temple. Engraving by Ignaz Alberti. 158 × 95mm.

WOLFGANG AMADEUS MOZART

DIE RACHE ER.
WARTET HIER
MEINEN MÖRDER

Ridotto per il Piano Forte da A. E. Müller

illustrations occur on the titlepages of group publications of various kinds. A set of six operas in vocal score was issued by the Parisian publisher Maurice Schlesinger about 1822. (This set is unusual in that all the vignettes on the titlepages are printed by lithography.) The delightful illustration of *Die Entführung aus dem Serail* depicts the midnight elopement scene at the beginning of Act 3 (fig.55). A similar set of six Mozart operas was issued in London by the very enterprising publisher D'Almaine at various dates from 1816 onwards. These are not in vocal score but in an arrangement for piano with violin and cello. Each number has a finely engraved vignette on the titlepage. That to *Così fan tutte* (fig.56) shows the two pairs of lovers in Act II Scene 3. There is some reason for thinking that the vignettes in this whole set were based on the designs for the early productions of the operas given at the King's Theatre, Haymarket.

As with the illustrations of *Don Giovanni*, so with *Le nozze di Figaro* the same scene was often repeated – the discovery of Cherubino in the

52. Unsigned vignette of the churchyard scene in *Don Giovanni*, Act II Scene 11, from a vocal score of *c*.1810. Aquatint. 136 × 203mm.

53. Frontispiece to a vocal score of *La clemenza di Tito*, *c.*1795, showing the burning of the Capitol, Act 1 Scene 4. Engraving by Johann August Rosmässler. 268 × 292mm.

arm-chair in the Countess's room. A much less familiar one is found not in a musical score but in the 1827 issue of an annual pocket-book entitled *Orphea*. This shows the very opening of Act I of *Figaro*, where Susanna tries on her hat while Figaro measures the floor (fig.57). *Orphea* was typical of many small annuals issued in France and Germany during the early nineteenth century. Elegantly produced, neatly printed and well illustrated, they contained essays, poems, and sketches on a wide range of topics. *Orphea* is of unusual interest because the 1827 issue contains seven other vivid engravings of scenes in *Le Nozze di Figaro*, while the issues for 1825 and 1826 each contain eight similar engravings for *Don Giovanni* and *Die Zauberflöte* respectively. Each scene is identified by the musical incipit added below the engraving. Although none of these sets of engravings can be related to specific productions, they probably bear some relation to the eclectic style of costumes seen in German opera houses of the 1820s.

54. Vignette of
Act II Scene 6 in
Idomeneo, from a
vocal score of
c.1796.
Engraving by
C. Seipp.
90 × 132mm.

55. Vignette of the elopement scene in *Die Entführung aus dem Serail*, Act III Scene 1, from a vocal score of *c.* 1822. Lithograph by Gottfried Engelmann. 150 × 165mm.

56. (*Left*) Vignette of Act 2 Scene 3 in *Così fan tutte*, from an instrumental arrangement of *c.* 1818. Stipple by James Hopwood. 116 × 140mm.

Undoubtedly the most magnificent set of designs ever published for any Mozart opera is that for *Die Zauberflöte* by Karl Friedrich Schinkel, the famous German architect, stage designer and painter who was appointed to the Royal Theatre in Berlin in 1815. The principles underlying his work for this opera and some forty other operas and ballets were innovatory. Because the whole stage had to be visible from the auditorium, there could be no flats, and the design took the form of a huge backcloth in front of which the action took place. Schinkel's eight designs for *Die Zauberflöte* were used in the monumental Berlin production of 1816. While the style is a highly individual blend of the neo-classical and the early romantic, they are unique in brooding, imaginative power, as exemplified in the one reproduced as plate IV.

57. *Le nozze di Figaro*, Act 1 Scene 1. From *Orphea. Taschenbuch*, 1827.
Engraved by Carl August Schwerdgeburth after Johann Heinrich Ramberg.
132 × 90mm.

On 11 March 1828 Johann Peter Eckermann recorded one of his famous conversations with Goethe, who remarked that he detected in Mozart 'a latent, procreative force which is continuously effective from generation to generation, and is not likely soon to be exhausted'. Goethe was probably thinking of the 'force' revealed by Mozart's music in performance. But his words may also be considered in the context of a great collection such as that in the British Library – a 'legacy' which during the last century and a half has acquired a wealth of associations unimaginable in Goethe's day.

The original musical documents in Mozart's hand now have a fascination all their own. For they offer palpable evidence of his dynamic personality and embody the potency of his ideas expressed symbolically on paper. The illustrations of his operas shown in the preceding pages give a sample of the vivid ideas which these works evoked from artists employed by publishers and from designers working in the theatre. In the early editions of Mozart's music posterity can see the elegant, stylish care lavished on the titlepages by contemporary publishers, some of whom were his friends, and by their immediate successors to whom he was still a living memory. The copious Mozart literature reflects the inexhaustible attraction which he has had for authors of many kinds, all well represented in the British Library – collectors, bibliographers, essayists, writers of fiction, children's books, and plays. Far more extensive and substantial is the work produced by critics and biographers, who have responded to the challenge of the intellectual and emotional ambiguity of Mozart's music, and have tried to penetrate the mystery of his genius and its universality. The 'force' which has generated such prolonged, diverse activity will surely continue undiminished, as Goethe predicted.

List of Manuscripts in the British Library

Note: Except where otherwise stated, all manuscripts are in the collections of the Department of Manuscripts.

I. *Manuscripts in Mozart's hand*

(a) Autograph music (arranged according to Köchel numbers)

Four-part chorus, *God is our Refuge*. K20. (Music Library.) K.10.a.17.(1). (Partly in Mozart's hand, partly in his father's.)

Cadenza for a concerto movement for piano and orchestra, adapted from a sonata by Leontzi Honauer. K40. Add. MS 47861A f.10r.

String quartet in F major. K168. Fragment of a possibly earlier version of the minuet, K168a. Add. MS 47861A f.10v.

String quartet in B flat major. K172. Add. MS 31749.

String quartet in D minor. K173. Draft of part of the last movement. Loan 42/9.

Minuet, no.3, and trio, no.6, of a set of dances for orchestra. K176. Arranged for piano. Add. MS 14396, f.13.

Two cadenzas for the first and second movements of the piano concerto in C major. K246. 1b and 2b. Add. MS 61905.

Sonata for piano duet in B flat major. K358. Add. MS 14396, ff.22–29v.

Sonata for violin and piano in F major. K377. Loan 42/13.

Rondo for piano and orchestra in A major. K386. A fragment, comprising the last forty-five bars of the score. Add. MS 32181, ff.250r–252v.

String quartet in G major. K387. Add. MS 37763, ff.1–13v.

String quintet in C minor. K406/516b. Add. MS 31748, ff.15–27.

March for orchestra in C major. K408 no.1/383e. Loan 42/10.

String quartet in D minor. K421/417b. Add. MS 37763, ff.14–22v.

String quartet in E flat major. K428/421b. Add. MS 37763, ff.34–44r.

Concerto for horn and orchestra in E flat major. K447. Loan 42/7.

String quartet in B flat major. K458. Add. MS 37763, ff.23–33v.

String quartet in A major. K464. Add. MS 37763, 45–56v.

String quartet in C major. K465. Add. MS 37763, 57–68v.

Song, *Das Veilchen*. K476. Loan 42/4.

Draft of the aria 'Non so più', in *Le nozze di Figaro*. K492. Loan 42/8.

Sketches for themes in the finale of the piano quartet in E flat major. K493. (Music Library.) K.6.e.2. f.17v.

String quartet in D major. K499. Add. MS 37764.

The Attwood manuscript, with numerous corrections in Mozart's hand and two minuets composed by him. K506a. Add. MS 58437.

Eight textless canons. K508a. (Music Library.) K.6.e.2. f.17v.

Adagio and fugue for string quartet in C minor. K546. (Only the Adagio in Mozart's hand.) Add. MS 28966.

Canon, *Difficile lectu mihi Mars*. K559. Canon, *O du eselhafter Peierl*, K560a. Loan 42/12.

Piano sonata in B flat major. K570. (One leaf only of the first movement.) Add. MS 48761A, f.13.

String quartet in D major. K575. Add. MS 37765, ff.1–14v.

String quartet in B flat major. K589. Add. MS 37765, ff.29–44v.

String quartet in F major. K590. Add. MS 37765, ff.15–28v.

Five contredanses for orchestra. K609. Loan 42/11.

String quintet in E flat major. K614. Loan 42/5.

Quintet for armonica, flute, oboe, viola and violoncello. K617. Loan 42/6.

Duettino, 'Deh prendi un dolce amplesso', in *La clemenza di Tito*. K621. Loan 42/14.

Note: the autograph score of the concerto for piano and orchestra in C minor, K491, which was deposited on loan in 1946 by the Royal College of Music, was returned to the College in 1961.

(b) Copies by Mozart of music by other composers

Ave Maria in F major, by Johann Michael Haydn. KAnh. A14. Add. MS 41633, ff.60–63v.

Finale of a symphony in D major by Johann Michael Haydn. KAnh. A52. Loan 79/6.

De profundis clamavi in C minor, by Carl Georg Reutter. KAnh. A22. Add. MS 31748.

(c) Autograph documents and letters

'Verzeichnüss aller meiner Werke. . .' (Mozart's thematic catalogue, 1784–1791.) Loan 42/1.

Four letters to his cousin, Maria Anna Thekla Mozart. 5 November 1777, 28 February 1778, 23 December 1778, 10 May 1779. Loan 42/3.

Letter to Professor Anton Klein. 21 May 1785. Loan 42/3.

Letter to his sister, Maria Anna von Berchtold zu Sonnenburg, 19 December 1787. Add. MS 41628, ff.204–204b.

Contract of marriage between Wolfgang Amadeus Mozart and Constanze Weber, Vienna, 3 August 1782. Signed by the bridegroom and bride; by the bride's mother Maria Cecilia Weber; and by Johann Thorwart (the bride's guardian), Johann Carl Cetto von Kronstorff, and Franz Gilowsky as witnesses. Loan 42/2.

II. Autographs of other members of the Mozart family

Four-part contrapuntal exercise by Leopold Mozart. K626b/39. Add. MS 14396, f.14.

Copies by Leopold Mozart of eighteen pieces of church music, two composed by Johann Michael Haydn, the rest by Johann Ernst Eberlin. KAnh. A71–88. Add. MS 41633, ff.1–59, 64–77.

Letter from Leopold Mozart to his daughter, Maria Anna von Berchtold zu Sonnenburg, February 1786. Add. MS 41628, ff.202–203v.

An arpeggio exercise possibly in the hand of Maria Anna Mozart. Loan 79/5.

Letter from Constanze Nissen to — Sattler. 30 April 1835. Add. MS 47843, f.35.

Aria buffo by Mozart's younger son Franz Xaver Wolfgang Mozart. Op.13. 1808. Add. MS 14396, f.1–12v.

III. Copies of Mozart's works by others (selective)

Copy, by Leopold Mozart, 1764, of the violin part to the printed sonatas for violin and piano. K10–15. (Music Library.) R.M.11.f.5.

Copy, by Vincent Novello, 1832, of *God is our Refuge*. K20. Add. MS 61949.

Copy, by Laurent Lausch, *c.*1790, of the aria 'Al desio, di chi t'adora', K577, preceded by the recitative 'Giunse al fin', from *Le nozze di Figaro*, and followed by a short cadenza in Mozart's hand. Add. MS 14396. f.21v.

Copies, by unidentified copyists of the late eighteenth century, of the following operas in full score, presented to the British Museum by Domenico Dragonetti:

  Ascanio in Alba   Add. MSS 16051, 16052
  La clemenza di Tito   Add. MSS 16053, 16054
  Le nozze di Figaro   Add. MSS 16055, 16056
  Lucio Silla   Add. MS 16057
  Mitridate, rè di Ponto   Add. MS 16058
  Idomeneo   Add. MSS 16059–61

Copies, by unidentified copyists of the late eighteenth century, of the following operas in full score, all of unknown provenance and now in the Royal Music Library (Music Library):

Così fan tutte   R.M. 22.h.10,11
La clemenza di Tito   R.M. 22.h.12,13
Die Entführung aus dem Serail   R.M. 22.h.14,15
Die Zauberflöte   R.M. 22.h.16,17
Le nozze di Figaro   R.M. 22.i.3–5
Idomeneo   R.M. 22.i.6–8.

Sources and Literature

General

The following books are the primary sources for details of Mozart's life and background as mentioned selectively in the preceding pages: *Mozart. Briefe und Aufzeichnungen. Gesamtausgabe Herausgegeben von der Internationalen Stiftung Mozarteum Salzburg.* Gesammelt und erläutert von Wilhelm A. Bauer und Otto Erich Deutsch (auf Grund deren Vorarbeiten erläutert von Joseph Heinz Eibl), 7 vol., Bärenreiter, Kassel, 1962–75. Vols.1–4 comprise the text, vols.5,6 the commentary, and vol.7 the index. Eibl was responsible for vols.5,6 and 7. This collection – *M.B.A.* – which is entirely in German, includes the complete text of everything written by any member of the Mozart family from 1755 up to 1850 – letters, diaries and many other kinds of document.

The first scholarly edition in English of the epistolary part of these sources was: *The Letters of Mozart and his Family. Chronologically arranged, translated and edited with an introduction, notes and indices by Emily Anderson. With extracts from the letters of Constanze Mozart to Johann Anton André.* Translated and edited by C. B. Oldman, 3 vol., Macmillan, London, 1938. This edition includes only letters written in Mozart's lifetime. While all Mozart's letters are given complete, there are only extracts of those written by his father and mother. Constanze's letters bear closely on the transmission of Mozart's autographs. Macmillan published a two-volume second edition of the Anderson translation in 1966, in a limited revision by A. Hyatt King and Monica Carolan, omitting Constanze Mozart's letters to André.

The essential complementary book to the preceding is: *Mozart. A documentary biography.* By Otto Erich Deutsch. Translated by Eric Blom, Peter Branscombe and Jeremy Noble, A. & C. Black, London, 1965. It presents, in chronological order, documents of every imaginable kind (excluding the family's letters) from 1755 up to 1891, which have any direct bearing on Mozart's life and works. A German supplement, *Mozart. Die Dokumente seines Lebens. Addenda und Corrigenda zusammengestellt von Joseph Heinz Eibl,* was issued by Bärenreiter in 1978.

The visual background can be found in two books: *Mozart und seine Welt in zeitgenössischen Bildern. Begründet von Maximilian Zenger, vorgelegt von Otto Erich Deutsch.* Bärenreiter, Kassel, 1961, and Robert Bory's *La vie et l'oeuvre de Wolfgang-Amadeus Mozart par l'image.* Les editions contemporains; Genève, 1948. In the former, the captions and notes are in German and

English; the latter is solely in French. To some extent Bory's book is duplicated by Deutsch's, but much of the topography is different, as is also the choice of Mozart's musical autographs in facsimile. The quality of Bory's reproductions is notably high.

The standard editions of Mozart's music are mentioned in the notes to Chapter 6.

The evolution of Mozart's musical handwriting, its relation to his father's and the consequent problems of authenticity, are complex topics. The best discussion of them is in three articles by Wolfgang Plath, all in the *Mozart-Jahrbuch:* 'Beiträge zur Mozart-Autographie I: Die Handschrift Leopold Mozarts', 1960–61, pp.82–117; 'Zur Echtsheitfrage bei Mozart', 1971–72, pp.19–36; 'Beiträge zur Mozart-Autographie II: Schriftchronologie 1770–1780', 1976–77, pp.131–173. Much of this research has affected the dating of certain works, particularly those composed up to the early 1770s. (See the notes to Chapter 3.) The Stefan Zweig collection of Mozart autographs, which are mentioned in Chapters 3, 4 and 5, comprise Loan 42 and are all included in the List on pp.92–4. In his autobiography, translated into English as *The World of Yesterday* (Cassell, London, 1943), Zweig himself gave, on pp.264–8, a most interesting account of the principles and sentiments which informed his collecting of autographs, literary as well as musical.

1. The Mozart Gift

The origin of the British Museum and its library, and the state of the collections at the time of the Mozarts' visit are described in *The British Museum Library. A short history and survey,* by Arundell Esdaile (Allen & Unwin, London, 1946, second impression 1948), and in *That Noble Cabinet. A history of the British Museum,* by Edward Miller (André Deutsch, London, 1973). The architecture of Montagu House, its gradual replacement by Smirke's building and the relation of both to the collections, are discussed with insight by J. Mordaunt Crook in *The British Museum* (Allen Lane, the Penguin Press, London, 1972).

For the relation of the Mozart gift to the collections of music, the reader may consult *Printed Music in the British Museum,* by Alec Hyatt King (Clive Bingley, London, 1979). The pages of Leopold Mozart's travel diary written during his stay in London are included in the facsimile edition of the whole, *Leopold Mozart. Reise-Aufzeichnungen 1763–1771. Herausgegeben und erläutert von Arthur Schurig.* (Oscar Laube: Dresden, 1920). Musical life in London in the 1760s is described in C. F. Pohl's *Mozart in London* [in German], Vienna, 1867. Though superseded in some details by later research, this is still the most comprehensive account. But its spelling of English names and words is defective.

Carmontelle's painting of Leopold Mozart and Wolfgang alone is illustrated on the cover of the catalogue of a Bibliothèque Nationale exhibition, *Mozart en France*, Paris, 1956.

2. Vincent Novello and the Mozart Family

The source for the Novellos' visit to Salzburg is: *A Mozart Pilgrimage. Being the travel diaries of Vincent & Mary Novello in the year 1829*. Transcribed and compiled by Nerina Medici di Marignano. Edited by Rosemary Hughes, Novello & Co., London, 1955. Most of the text of Novello's proposal to establish a proper music library in the British Museum is quoted in: *Printed Music in the British Museum*, by Alec Hyatt King, 1979, pp.25–6. The full proposal, with other related papers, is in the Music Library, pressmark K.5.b.8.

The autograph of the duet sonata K358 was owned by four people after Mozart's sister gave it away and before it passed to Novello. One of them, Miss Tomkison, remains obscure. But a tentative identification of the other three is possible. In the list of subscribers to Nissen's biography of Mozart there appears (p.xxxvii) a firm of London booksellers 'Black, Young et Young'. Some of their catalogues now in the British Library show that they specialised in German literature, and the two latter members of this firm can perhaps be identified with Charles and Winslow Young. It seems likely that 'Mrs Lydia Hunt' was a member of Leigh Hunt's family, who were close friends of the Novellos. A Mrs. Blaine Hunt appears in the Novello family portrait which was painted by Edward Novello (d.1836) and is reproduced opposite p.30 in Averil Mackenzie-Grieve's *Clara Novello*, Geoffrey Bles, London, 1955. In her treatise *Observations on the vocal Shake*, which was published by Novello in 1837 with a dedication to his daughter Cecilia, she describes herself as 'Professor of Singing'. Her identity with Lydia Hunt seems to be established by the pencil signature 'L. B. Hunt' which is faintly legible on f.29v of the autograph of K358.

3. The Chamber Music Autographs

Mozart's methods of composition, the nature of the corrections and cancellations in the autographs of the ten quartets, and their relation to extant sketches on separate leaves are all complicated matters which lie beyond the scope of this book. They are discussed by a number of scholars in the following volume: *The String Quartets of Haydn, Mozart, and Beethoven. Studies of the autograph manuscripts. A conference at the Isham Memorial Library, March 15–17, 1979*, edited by Christoph Wolff, Harvard University Press, 1980 (Isham Library Papers III). The four Mozart contributors were

Ludwig Finscher, 'Aspects of Mozart's compositional process in the Quartet Autographs. I. The early quartets (including K172). II. The Genesis of K387'; Marius Flothuis, 'A close Reading of the Autographs of Mozart's ten late Quartets'; Alan Tyson, 'Mozart's Quartets: the contribution of paper studies'; Christoph Wolff, 'Creative Exuberance vs. critical choice: Thoughts on Mozart's Quartet Fragments'. Tyson has also written two other essays of immediate relevance to the autographs in the British Library – 'The Origins of Mozart's "Hunt" Quartet, K458', in *Music and Bibliography. Essays in honour of Alec Hyatt King*, edited by O. W. Neighbour, Saur/Bingley, London, 1980, pp.133–48; and 'New Light on Mozart's Prussian Quartets', *Musical Times*, cxvi, 1975, pp.126–130.

The story of Speyer's intervention in the matter of Mozart's 'ten quartets' was published in Edward Speyer's *My Life and Friends*, Cobden-Sanderson, London, 1937, pp.208–9. The nature of the first editions of these works and their textual relation to the autographs is fully discussed in: *W. A. Mozart. The ten celebrated quartets. First authentic edition in score*, edited by Alfred Einstein, Novello & Co, London, 1945. The German text of Einstein's introduction and critical notes is printed in parallel with an English translation, probably made by C. B. Oldman. The autograph scores of all ten quartets were published in facsimile by the Robert Owen Lehman Foundation, New York, in 1969. The leaf which contained part of the minuet K168a (and, on the reverse, the cadenza for the Honauer concerto movement) is discussed by E. F. Schmid in an article in the *Mozart-Jahrbuch 1957*, pp.43–56, 'Schicksale einer Mozart-Handschrift. Ein unbekanntes Streichquartett-Menuet und zwei unveröffentlichte Kadenzen'. Schmid reconstructs, in facsimile, both sides of the leaf as it was before Constanze Mozart cut it up.

Mozart's drafts for the finale of K493 are published in *N.M.A.* VIII, 22, Abt.1, pp.160,167. The Wandering Minstrels, a Victorian amateur musical society, are discussed in two articles by A. Hyatt King: 'Einstein, Oldman and the Wandering Minstrels', *Musical Times*, March 1984, pp. 145–8 and 'The Wandering Minstrels and their Archive', in *Ars iocundissima, Festschrift für Kurt Dorfmüller*, ed. Horst Leuchtmann, Tutzing, 1984, pp.167–178.

The armonica, for which Mozart composed the quintet K617, has now largely fallen into disuse. But this work has become well known in the last fifty years through the masterly performances of Bruno Hoffmann, who has preferred to use the musical glasses, from which originally the armonica was developed. His autobiography, *Ein Leben für die Glasharfe*, Niederland-Verlag, Backnang, 1983, gives an excellent account of both instruments, with many illustrations.

4. Other Mozart Works in Autograph

Regarding the fragmentary autograph of Mozart's Rondo in A, K386, W. Warde Fowler, in his *Stray Notes on Mozart and his Music* (privately printed under his initials, W.W.F., Edinburgh, 1910), mentions, on pp.9–10, how in 1860 he came across two of the leaves, then owned by an Oxford friend, Thomas Case, son-in-law of Sterndale Bennett and later President of Corpus. Fowler tried to persuade Sir John Stainer to produce an orchestral version of the work, based on these leaves and Potter's arrangement. The latter is discussed in its full context in an article by C. B. Oldman, 'Cipriani Potter's Edition of Mozart's Pianoforte Works', *Festschrift für Otto Erich Deutsch zum 80. Geburtstag*. Herausgegeben von Walter Gerstenberg, Jan La Rue, und Wolfgang Rehm, Bärenreiter, Kassel, 1963, pp.120–7. This *Festschrift* also has an article by Rehm, pp.140–151, 'Miscellanea Mozartiana II', which reprints with full commentary Gustav André's London catalogue of the autographs.

5. Miscellaneous Autographs and Documents

Verzeichnüss aller meiner Werke. . .

This document was first published in facsimile by Herbert Reichner Verlag, Vienna, in 1938, with an accompanying booklet by Otto Erich Deutsch, in German, entitled *Mozarts Werkverzeichnis*. In 1956 the same firm reissued the facsimile in New York, with Deutsch's booklet in an English version, *Mozart's Catalogue of his Works*. The facsimile is slightly reduced from the original, and a number of marks and other details written close to the outer margins have been lost. It also omits the significant blank leaves.

Two American scholars, Daniel N. Leeson, and David Whitwell, discussed this document in an important article, 'Mozart's Thematic Catalogue', *Musical Times*, August 1973, pp.781–3. From external evidence they show that the dates which Mozart gave to most of the first ten entries were written retrospectively and need revision. They also suggest that Mozart began the catalogue at a time of crisis about November 1784 when his recovery from serious illness coincided with remembrance of the death of an infant son a year before, so making him aware of his own mortality, which again may be reflected in his entering a Masonic lodge at this same time.

The Attwood Manuscript

This was published complete in 1965 as part of the *Neue Mozart Ausgabe* (Series X, Supplement, Band 1), under the title 'Thomas Attwoods Theorie- und Kompositionsstudien bei Mozart' prepared by Erich Hertzmann and C. B. Oldman, and finally edited by Daniel Hertz and Alfred

Mann. The introduction and the long 'Kritische Bericht' are in German only. Attwood's exercises and remarks are printed in black, while Mozart's corrections, additions and remarks are in red. This manuscript is the subject of two articles by its one-time owner, C. B. Oldman – 'Thomas Attwood's Studies with Mozart', *Gedenkbuch aangeboden aan Dr. D. F. Scheurleer* ('s Gravenhage, 1925), pp.227–240, and 'Two Minuets by Attwood, with corrections by Mozart', *Music Review,* 1946, pp.166–9.

The Copies

For the details of the handwriting of the Mozarts, father and son, see the articles by Plath cited on p.97.

The Letters

The German text of Mozart's letters to his cousin is included in *Mozart. Briefe und Aufzeichnungen.* There have also been some separate editions, of which the most recent is: *Mozarts Bäsle-Briefe.* Herausgegeben und kommentiert von Joseph Heinz Eibl und Walter Senn. Mit Vorwort von Wolfgang Hildesheimer, 2nd edition, Bärenreiter, Kassel, 1982. A full English translation of these letters was included in Emily Anderson's *Letters of Mozart and his Family* (1938, second edition 1966.) In his *Mozart,* translated from the German by Marion Faber, J. M. Dent, London, 1983, Hildesheimer discusses them at inordinate length. The scanty facts about Mozart's cousin will be found in a little book by Ludwig Wegele, *Der Lebenslauf der Marianne Thekla Mozart,* Verlag Die Brigg, Augsburg, 1967, for the German Mozart Society.

A possible autograph by 'Nannerl' Mozart

I am indebted to Dr. Plath for the attribution of the arpeggio exercise to 'Nannerl' Mozart.

6. From Manuscript to Print

The first complete critical edition of Mozart's music was published in parts by Breitkopf & Härtel, the bulk of its twenty-three series between 1877 and 1883, with a supplement of sixty-one items issued at intervals up to 1905. Full details, with the date of each part, are given in pp.925–33 of the sixth edition of Köchel. The *Neue Mozart Ausgabe* began to appear, planned in thirty-five 'Werkgruppe', under Bärenreiter's imprint, in 1955 and by 1984 had reached 100 volumes out of an expected total of about 120.

The early publication of Mozart's works is described in two articles by O. E. Deutsch and C. B. Oldman in *Die Zeitschrift für Musikwissenschaft,* Jahrg. 14, 1931–32: 'Mozart-Drucke. Eine bibliographische Ergänzung zu

Köchels Werkverzeichnis' – 'I. Die zu Mozarts Lebzeiten erschienenen Drucke', pp.136–150, and 'II. Die für Mozart-Drucke verwendeten Opuszahlen', pp.337–351. Subsequent discoveries have not added substantially to these lists.

Leopold Mozart's list of his son's early compositions was published as: *Leopold Mozart. Werkverzeichnis für Wolfgang Amadeus Mozart (1768). Ein Beitrag zur Mozartforschung.* Eingeleitet und herausgegeben von Karl Franz Müller, Pallas Verlag, Salzburg, 1955. This includes a complete facsimile. The list was also printed in *M.B.A.*, vol.1.

The article on Johann Anton André in *The New Grove Dictionary of Music*, written by Wolfgang Plath, gives an authoritative account of his importance in the preservation and transmission of the sources of Mozart's music and describes the earlier work of Franz Gleissner. For a description of André's thematic catalogue of 1833, see an article by C. B. Oldman, 'J. A. André on Mozart's manuscripts', *Music and Letters*, 1924, pp.169–76. This includes a translation of André's preface. The whole manuscript was then believed to be in André's hand, having been purchased as such by the British Museum in 1884 (Add. MS 32142). It is in fact a copy, in an unknown hand or hands, and was once owned by Jahn, in the sale catalogue of whose library it appeared in 1870. But as André's original autograph (which his heirs lent to Köchel) is now lost, this copy, the only one now known, is of unique value. Wolfgang Plath's seminal article, 'Chronologie als Problem der Mozartforschung', *Kongressbericht Bayreuth 1981*, Bärenreiter, Kassel, 1983, pp.371–8, includes a long discussion of André's catalogue of 1833 and his previous efforts in their full historical context.

The finale of the string quintet K593 is discussed by Ernst Hess, 'Die "Varianten" im Finale des Streichquintettes KV593', *Mozart-Jahrbuch*, 1960–61, pp.68–77.

Such significant thematic catalogues of composers as had appeared before Köchel referred solely to the first editions. All were published by Breitkopf – e.g. Mendelssohn (1846), Beethoven (1851), Chopin (1852). The second edition of Köchel's Mozart catalogue appeared in 1905, edited by Count Paul Waldersee. Though it contained some more information and references, it made little change in the numbering. Alfred Einstein, however, made many drastic alterations to it when preparing the third edition, which was issued in 1937. Einstein himself prepared a supplement of corrections and additions, which appeared in *The Music Review*, vols.1–6, 1940–1945. This supplement was not, however, included in the two reprints of the 1937 edition which were subsequently published in Leipzig as the fourth and fifth editions. The hugely expanded sixth edition, edited by Franz Giegling, Alexander Weinmann and Gerd Sievers, was published by Breitkopf & Härtel, Wiesbaden, in 1964.

Wolfgang Plath's three articles relating to Mozart's handwriting, and their bearing on chronology and authenticity, are cited on p.97.

Further details about Paul Hirsch are given in my article on him in *The New Grove Dictionary of Music,* and the literature there cited. Hirsch's two articles referred to in the text are: 'A Mozart Problem [the fantasia for piano in D minor]', *Music and Letters,* vol.25, 1944, pp.209–12; 'Ein unbekanntes Lied von W. A. Mozart (K552)', *Die Musik,* Jahrg.V, Bd.20, 1906, pp.164–5. Two more copies of this song have come to light since Hirsch's discovery.

Some further account of the origin of the title 'Jupiter' symphony is given in my book *Mozart in Retrospect,* Oxford University Press, 1955, revised edition 1970, p.263, where will also be found, on pp.261–2, more details of the large subscription list to *Così fan tutte.*

7. *Some Images of the Operas*

The growth in the popularity of Mozart's operas throughout Europe and America is documented in Alfred Loewenberg's *Annals of Opera, 1597–1940,* Heffer, Cambridge, 1943, third revised edition 1978.

The most detailed discussion of the masonic aspects of *Die Zauberflöte* is *The Magic Flute, masonic Opera. An interpretation of the libretto and the music,* by Jacques Chailley. Translated from the French by Herbert Weinstock, Gollancz, London, 1972. (Some of the author's ideas should be treated with caution.) The illustrated editions of the operas in the Hirsch Library are described in *Katalog der Musikbibliothek Paul Hirsch,* Band IV, 'Erstausgaben, Chorwerke in Partitur, etc', Cambridge University Press, 1947, throughout pp.3–302.

The illustrated editions issued by D'Almaine and other publishers are fully described in my article, 'Vignettes in early nineteenth-century London Editions of Mozart's Operas', *British Library Journal,* vol.6, no.1, Spring, 1980, pp.24–43.

Schinkel and his designs for *Die Zauberflöte* are discussed in an exhibition catalogue, *The Age of Neo-Classicism (The fourteenth exhibition of the Council of Europe),* Arts Council of Great Britain, 1972, pp.946–9. The article is signed 'MB', i.e. Manfred Boetkzes. Five of Schinkel's original gouaches were included in this exhibition.

Index